BEPPE GAMBETTA
guitar transcriptions

Blu di Genova

transcribed by Beppe Gambetta

MEL BAY PUBLICATIONS, INC., PACIFIC, MO 63069
© 2005 Beppe Gambetta. All Rights Reserved. Used By Permission.
Exclusive Sales Agent Mel Bay Publications, Inc., Pacific, MO 63069.
International Copyright Secured. B.M.I. Made and printed in U.S.A.

Visit us on the Web at www.melbay.com or www.billsmusicshelf.com

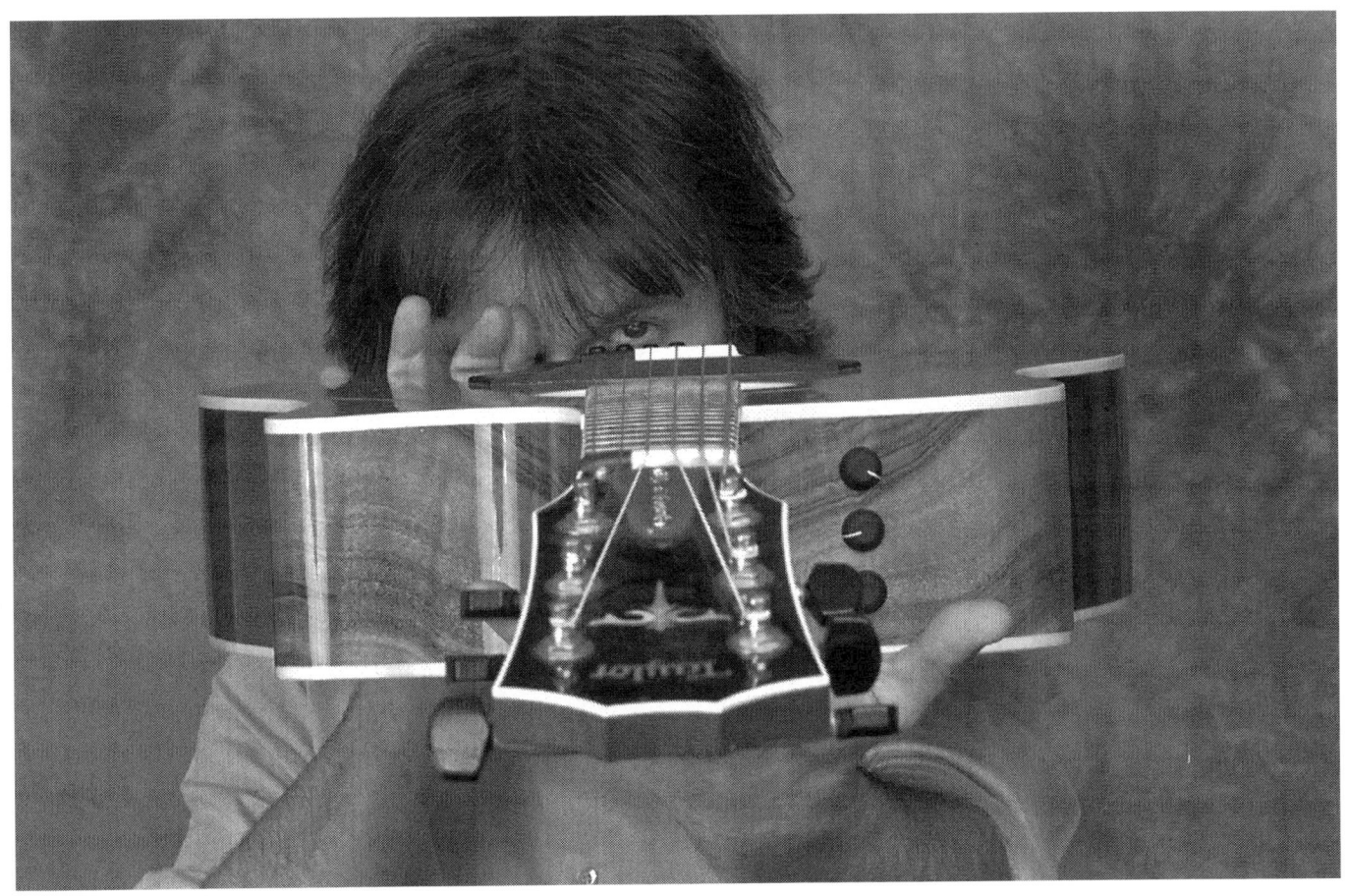

CONTENTS

INTRODUCTION	5
ON THE ROAD WITH MAMA	12
FANDANGO PER LA BIONDA	19
CHURCH STREET BLUES	24
SHENANDOAH VALLEY BREAKDOWN	28
A CIMMA	36
SESTRINA	38
A NIGHT IN FRONTENAC	43
NOVA GELOSIA	46
SERENATA	47
TARANTEXAS	51
FUINDE	57
MARCIA AMERICANA	64
UNDER THE DOUBLE EAGLE	71
RED SHOES	77

INTRODUCTION

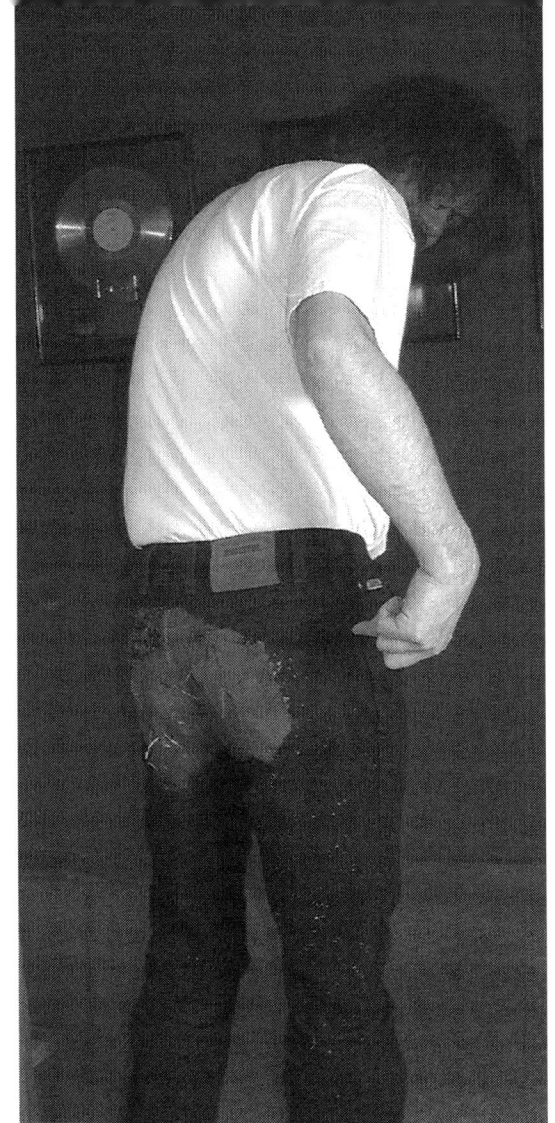

It was a perfect Oregon morning, flowers were blooming around the house at the top of the hill, the persistent rain of the previous days was gone, the sun was shining and Mount St. Helens was the highest point of a marvellous skyline. I said to Federica something like: "there is not a better place and moment to start the new album, this is a sign of good luck." We proceeded happily down the steep path to the studio with the guitar and the sketches for the new recording adventure in hand. I knew that Billy was waiting there with a cappuccino and this thought made me rush downhill not thinking of the last muddy part of the path until I found myself sliding down on my butt, covering myself with mud in order to save the guitar and generating unstoppable laughter from the whole company. In a pathetic effort to turn negative to positive, I said: "Mud made Woodstock unforgettable, it will be the same for the new album".

■ That was the beginning of **Blu di Genova**.
After years focusing my artistic activity on research and revival of some beautiful traditional musical forms, I had a strong need to go back to the natural creative role of acoustic guitar player, treasuring the latest experiences and involving in the process some of the old and new friends that music brought on my path in all those years. So, I'm going to tell some details about the itinerary of this production and give some introductions and comments about the individual pieces that will reach beyond the pure technical aspects.
At the beginning of the whole process there was the decision (not unusual in the independent music world) of how much money to spend for the production and how to take total control of it. You don't need to be particularly rich, you need only to be crazy and motivated enough towards music to spend all of your resources on your project. Then you will be able to say "I tried at least one time in my life to do it the way I wanted and how I think it should be done!" and this will allow you to walk into the pawn shop with much more dignity.

■ After that, there was great fun in inventing the concept for the album and choosing the place to work and the people to work with. In my case, I had been exposed to so much beauty generated by the American "melting pot" of cultures at the time of the great European emigrations that I wanted to recreate in my way this "migrating" vibe in this new production.
I decided to revolve the CD around this theme and move the project to be recorded back and forth on both sides of the Ocean to capture in present times a little hint of what is left of the old creative energy generated by this diversity.

■ From the sound point of view, I was fascinated with the deep acoustic response of the old analog technique and particularly from the results Billy Oskay was achieving in his "Big Red Studio" in Portland, Oregon using vintage Neumann microphones regenerated by Klaus Heine. So I did a lot of travelling by packing in my bag three giant reels of 24-track tapes that seemed to cause alarm among entire crews of security people, but after I listened to the musical result I think it was worth it to pass through all these troubles. So, if you are starting your project and you don't know how to spend some extra money and complicate your life, you should follow my example: this is a perfect windmill to aim for, with good artistic rewards.

■ I used two vintage Neumann microphones pointed on the body and the fretboard of my guitar, the main guitar I used was my Taylor K14 CE, a beautiful instrument in Koa wood with versatile tone and perfectly balanced sound. I used Elixir medium coated strings.
The CD was recorded in a few sessions, deciding after careful listening what to add and what to change, with many of the guest artists overdubbing separately their parts, due to the distance of the locations.

■ It was difficult to find the right title for this project and finally by exploring all the possible words to add to the word "blu", we stumbled into "Blu di Genova", the name of a fabric invented and produced several centuries ago in my hometown that, after a long evolution through France (Bleu de Genes) and a crossing on the other side of the Ocean, originated the word Bluejeans.
Nothing could be a better symbol of the positive and evolving relationship between the old and the new world, but still a lot of people things I'm joking when I tell this story.
I will have to bring some pictures from my hometown museum.

■ All the guitar parts of the album are transcribed in this book, and also the chords for the songs, I didn't write the text of the songs because all texts are easy to find with a simple internet search.
I don't like heavily simplified transcriptions. They are maybe more easy to learn but they lose part of the artistic sense that often is generated by little "hidden" embellishments, so I transcribed the whole guitar parts with accuracy and added a few simplifications just when it was necessary to clarify the structure of the piece.
Some tunes like the Fandango and A Night in Frontenac are conceived structurally as folk dance tunes. In these cases, the melody is repeated quite similarly in every run, with just some minor

variations in the intention and the dynamic.

For these tunes, in the transcription I decided not to repeat the "close to the same thing" many times and instead I represented in just one run the essence of the tune.

■ A live performance of eight numbers from "Blu di Genova" (tracks 1, 2, 3, 5, 6, 8, 10, 11) can be also seen on the newly produced DVD "Beppe Gambetta and Friends Live in Genova" by Mel Bay (MB#21150DVD).

The live versions are performed with fabulous guests and the guitar parts are very close to what I performed in the CD.

■ **On The Road With Mama** is a tune I obtained by overdubbing five different acoustic guitar voices (main part, "snare" guitar, "octaver" bass guitar, slide guitar, 12 string guitar counterpoints and harmonies) but, as is true in most of "Blu di Genova", the main guitar part (the one that I transcribed) is structured to be self-sufficient to be performed as a solo tune.

The main technical difficulty is to mantain a "rhytmic intensity" also in the parts played with multiple crosspicking solutions or intricate strumming directions.

A careful following of the suggested pick directions can be useful, although a good sound can be achieved with different personal solutions.

Advanced players will find the tune suitable to invent creative variations, particularly on the final runs of part B (for example measures 25 and 26) and a second guitar player could jam on the central more "free" part (from measure 64 to measure 91).

If you like to play On The Road With Mama with an ensemble, mandolin "chops" and a bass with stopped notes can suit the tune perfectly. For the slide parts, the guitar sounds good in open D.

If you perform it in Italy, because it becomes "On The Road With

MAMMA", you will have to leave late and drive at higher speed.

■ **Fandango Per La Bionda** is written to celebrate one of the Spanish dances that my wife Federica masters, in order to bring together our artistical paths. As happens often in every art, the creative process moved freely and the Fandango came out with an unusual slow mood and a minor first section that Fandango purists might find bizarre (but Freddy likes it and, at least to prove her love, she was brave to perform and dance while I was playing it).

The duet format with upright bass that plays in a far different range gives to the two instruments the fabulous opportunity to interact freely, moving without disturbing each other and maintaining a full sound. The jazz-world music view of Glen Moore was the perfect addition to match the guitar in the Fandango.

This tune shows how flatpicking is particularly well suited to perform dance music from different traditions. This should also inspire you to try your own experiment on some invented or revived dance tunes.

The most difficult technical part is the final phrase that needs precision while changing quickly from crosspicking to pull-off and hammer-on, and regular alternated strokes.

■ **Church Street Blues** is the quintessential "flatpicking related" song, composed by Norman Blake and revisited by Tony Rice. It was dangerous to change the song and add a new flavour.

I was made braver by a great contribution that came first from the lyrical harmony vocals of Gene Parsons. I also invented a new vamp with a progressive chord progression that allowed my guests to play tasty solos with instruments traditionally distant from the Flatpicking aesthetics. As a father, I love the moment when the progressive diatonic accordeon of my son Filippo touches my last solo.

Advanced players will have fun inventing variations on the vamp: the slow speed of this version facilitates the variety in the length of the notes from quarter notes to sixteen passing through any kind of triplet. This is particularly evident in the transcription of the solo of Dan Crary who played in E without capo some of his best "signature" licks.

If you like the rhythmic texture of the accompaniment in the album, you should notice that, besides guitar bass and percussions, there are sometimes interesting colours from a low-tuned bouzouki guitar.

In any case, the secret weapon in the creation of this complex arrangement was to relax by playing horse-shoe games between takes.

■ **Shenandoah Valley Breakdown** was a lot of fun to record: Banjo tunes are often borrowed by Flatpickers who like to reinvent in a "Flatpicking compatible mood" guitar licks that are reminiscent of the banjo roll. In order to get a little closer to the sound of the banjo, I decided to use the DADGAD tuning on this old standard that I heard many years ago from Bill Keith.

The duet with Dan was recorded strictly live without overdubbings. In this way the timing can be really tight in the switch from solo to accompaniment and well synchronized in the harmony parts.

Some of the accompaniment works really well if played by muting the strings with the palm (you gain strong intensity and clarity in the rhythm without covering the other guitar).

The arrangement is played around the contrast between improvised

solo licks and twin phrases in harmony and we couldn't resist to end it with a phrase in a "Newgrass" mood.

■ To accompany **A Cimma** I invented the DADEAE tuning (I later discovered that someone else previously already invented it!) where some chords have a particularly "evocative" sound.

The song is in Genovese dialect: a poetical ballad about the magical beauty in the traditional ritual of food. I indicated here the main chords shape to use in order to accompany the song. For the recipe you will need to consult a book of traditional Ligurian cuisine.

If you are a singer, the deep understanding of the song comes from listening to the original version of the poet-songwriter Fabrizio De André who wrote this song with Ivano Fossati (to listen to all the works of Fabrizio can be an enlightening experience for every artist).

■ The song is directly followed by the traditional **Sestrina**, ancient dance from the Appenini Mountains that I arranged by memory with some little changes as often happens in the traditional music.

In the guitar part, the major difficulties are in the control of the dynamics of the right hand because melody notes are often at the "top" of large strummings and need to be pushed "in front".
In the album, the guitar parts were completed by strummings and melody reinforcements of a 12 string guitar.

■ **A Night in Frontenac** is a duet that musically celebrates my friendship with Gene Parsons. The arrangement proves that you can also scat to embellish a flatpicking tune.

The composition is played around the contrast between the first more Old Timey- Folk part and a second more Bluesy section.
Sometimes while recording you experiment to blend unusual sounds and in this case it was fascinating to add the notes of an old harmonium over the final chords of the tune.

■ **Nova Gelosia / Serenata** follows the old tradition of the street serenaders of mixing different themes and songs in a romantic medley. It was a challenge to choose the notes for a guitar serenade to blend with the old Nova Gelosia, from many Centuries before.
The guitar part is conceived to work as a solo piece even without the support of the beautiful mandolin quartet parts of Carlo Aonzo.
The guitar structure of Serenata is a mix of the melody with an accompaning arpeggio that needs to be performed at lower volume.
The tune is a good laboratory to experience vibrato, long sustain and slow strumming and it is also possible to play it with breathing in the tempo.
Also in this case, listening to the historical version from the well known Neapolitan singer Roberto Murolo is the best way to inspire yourself for a romantic performance and learn the proper Neapolitan accent.

■ **Tarantexas** was composed some years ago as an attempt to find new modern expressions for the ancient Southern Italian dance. The inevitable contaminations of being on the road in Texas gave to the tune a good title and a peculiar "Tex-Southern Italian" flavour that Marco Fadda (the percussion player) was able to enhance by using the typical "Tamorra" tambourine played in elegant Southern style.
In the tune, I played with the pick parts that are often traditionally played with the fingers of the right hand in a sort of "rasgueado" style. The strummings need to be divided rhythmically in groups of strings, in order to create the typical triple time of the Southern dance. With all the basic movements, this one needs to be practiced alone to a fluent perfection and the whole tune will come together more easily.

■ **Fuinde** is meant to take the listener on another journey in the Mediterranean to the Island of Sardinia where ancient traditional guitar styles are still alive today.

I use partially the old techniques on the DGDGAD tuning (while in Sardinia the main traditional guitar tuning for this style is a low open C), thinking of the stories I heard from my Sardinian friend and luthier Antonello Saccu, running with his dog Ringo on this wild landscape.

The precise following of the "pick directions" can be really usefull for a fluid interpretation of the piece.

■ In the guitar and stringed instruments repertoire of the last Century, you can sometimes find some Marches performed by guitars. Guitar Marches from different cultures can fit together like this **Marcia Americana** (composed by the Italian virtuoso Pasquale Taraffo to celebrate the discovery of the guitar music of the New World he was visiting in 1929) together with the well known **Under the Double Eagle**. In the album I experimented the use of a tuba with a Flatpicking duo that turned out to drive delightfully the rhythm of the medley.

To hear some other similar melodies, I suggest you to listen to two of my previous CDs: "Serenata" (Acoustic Music Records, 1997) and "Traversata" (Acoustic Disc, 2001).

■ **Red Shoes** is my discrete walk away from the album in a muted fingerpicking style: 55 seconds of music will probably not get me a review in "Fingerstyle Guitar Magazine," but I love the idea of not being strictly associated just with one style of picking. Although Flatpicking is the style I use most prevalently, I rather prefer to be considered just an acoustic guitar player and composer and an artist who can also sing and arrange inspired by some great traditions from different parts of the world. This little tune proves also another important thing: if you make a mistake, and it sounds good, leave it there and maybe repeat it (like I did in measure 19): the listeners will think you are a "creative" composer.

This normally should be a secret, but we are in a teaching book and my students deserve this final confidence.

The copying of this transcriptions in the Finale 2003 format was done with accuracy by guitarist Roberto Dalla Vecchia (be sure to check out his great picking).

With this book of transcriptions I hope to give you inspirations, to introduce you to a different technical approach and to show you my enthusiasm for acoustic guitar music.

Ciao
Beppe Gambetta ♪

On The Road With Mama
Music by Beppe Gambetta

Tuning: D A D G A D

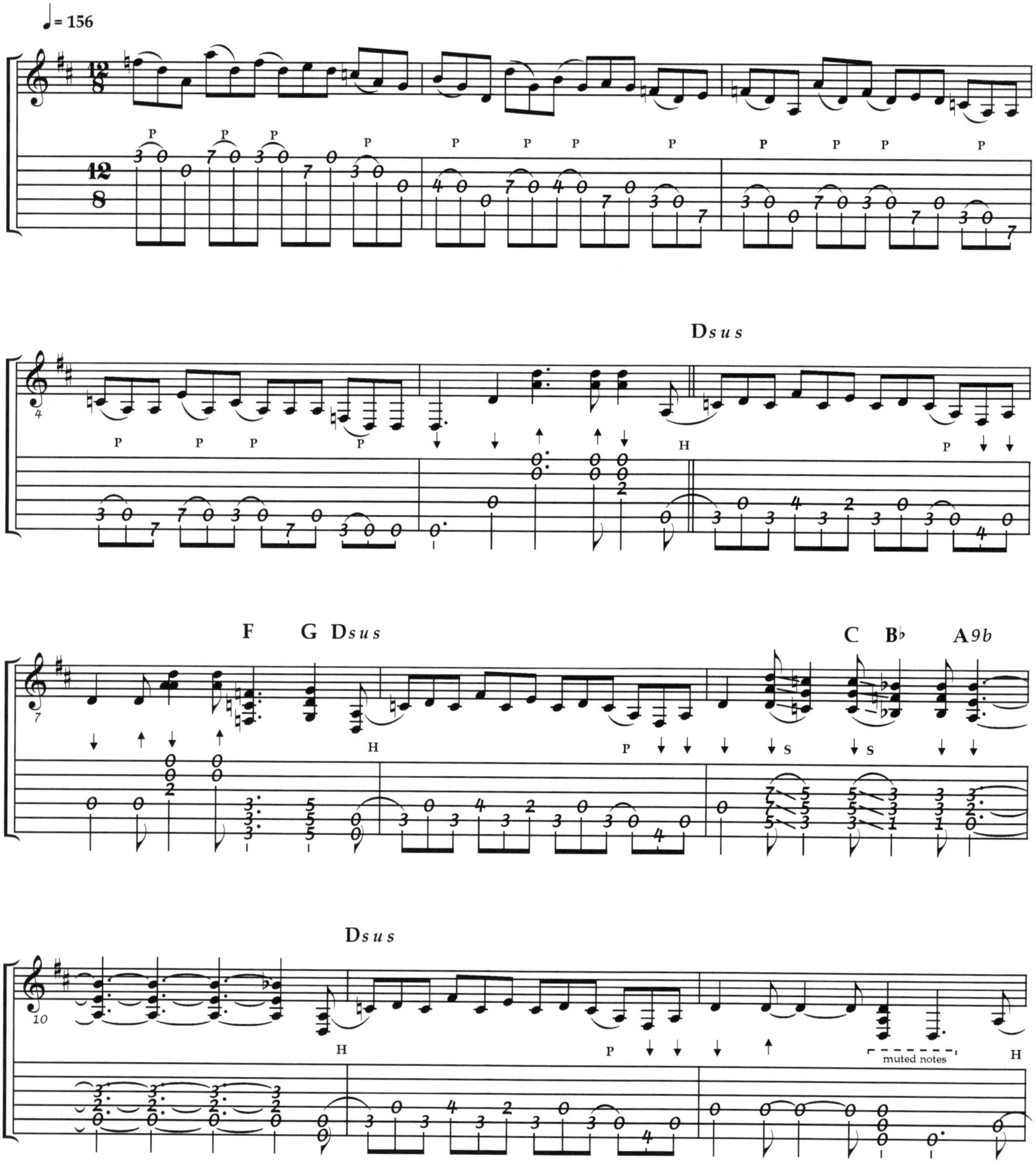

© 2002 Giuseppe Gambetta (SIAE - ITALY). All rights reserved. Used by permission.

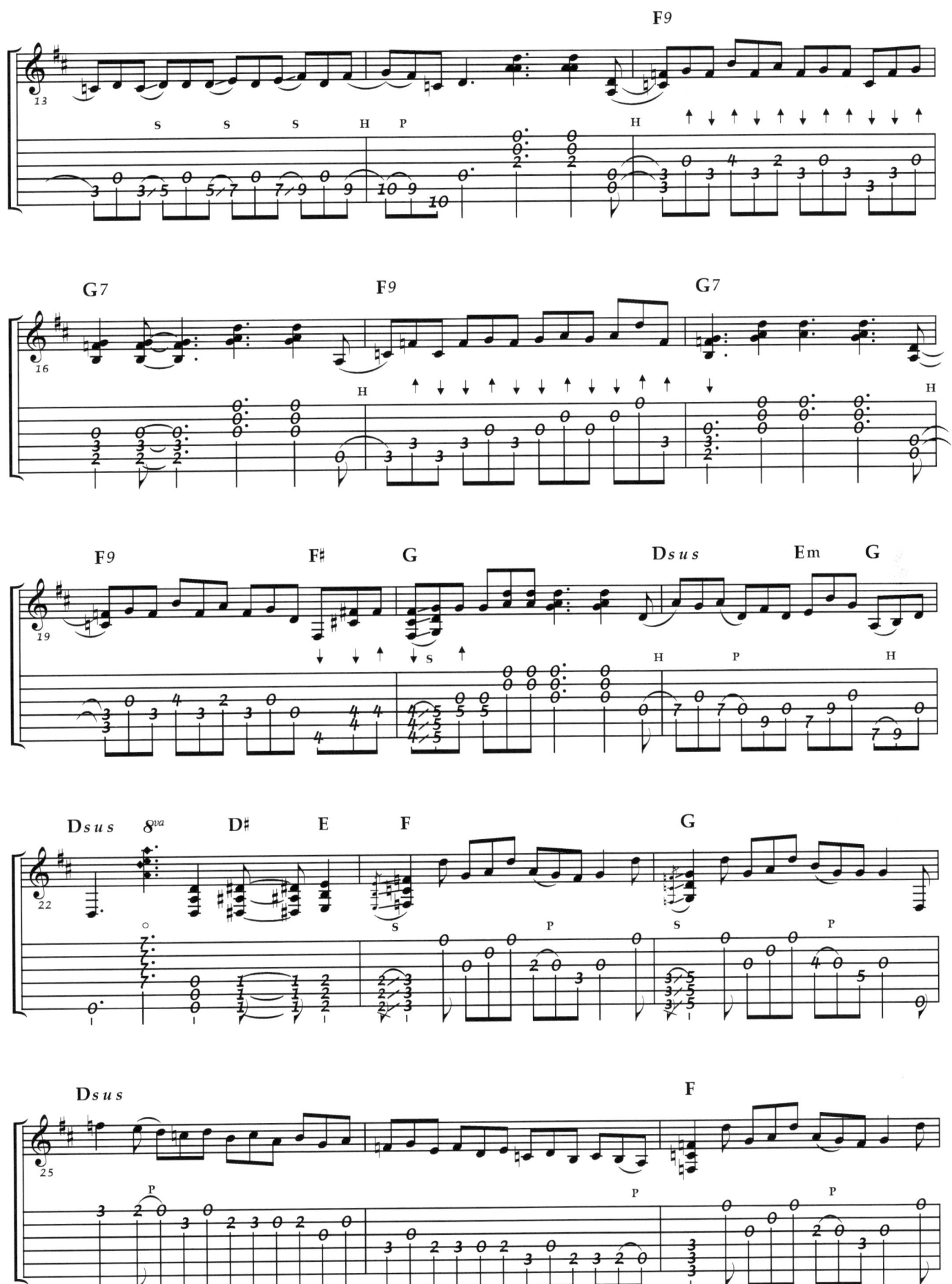

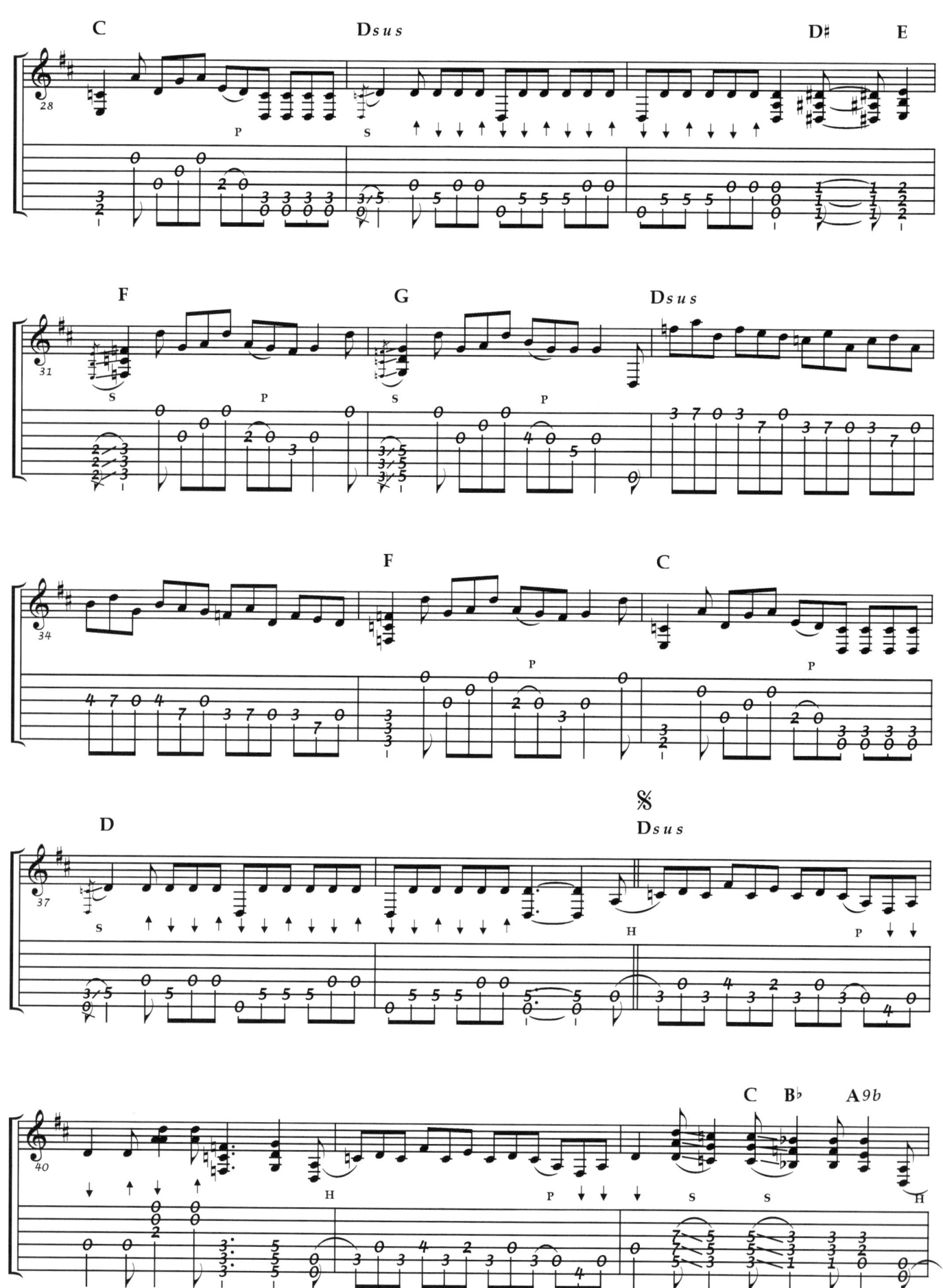

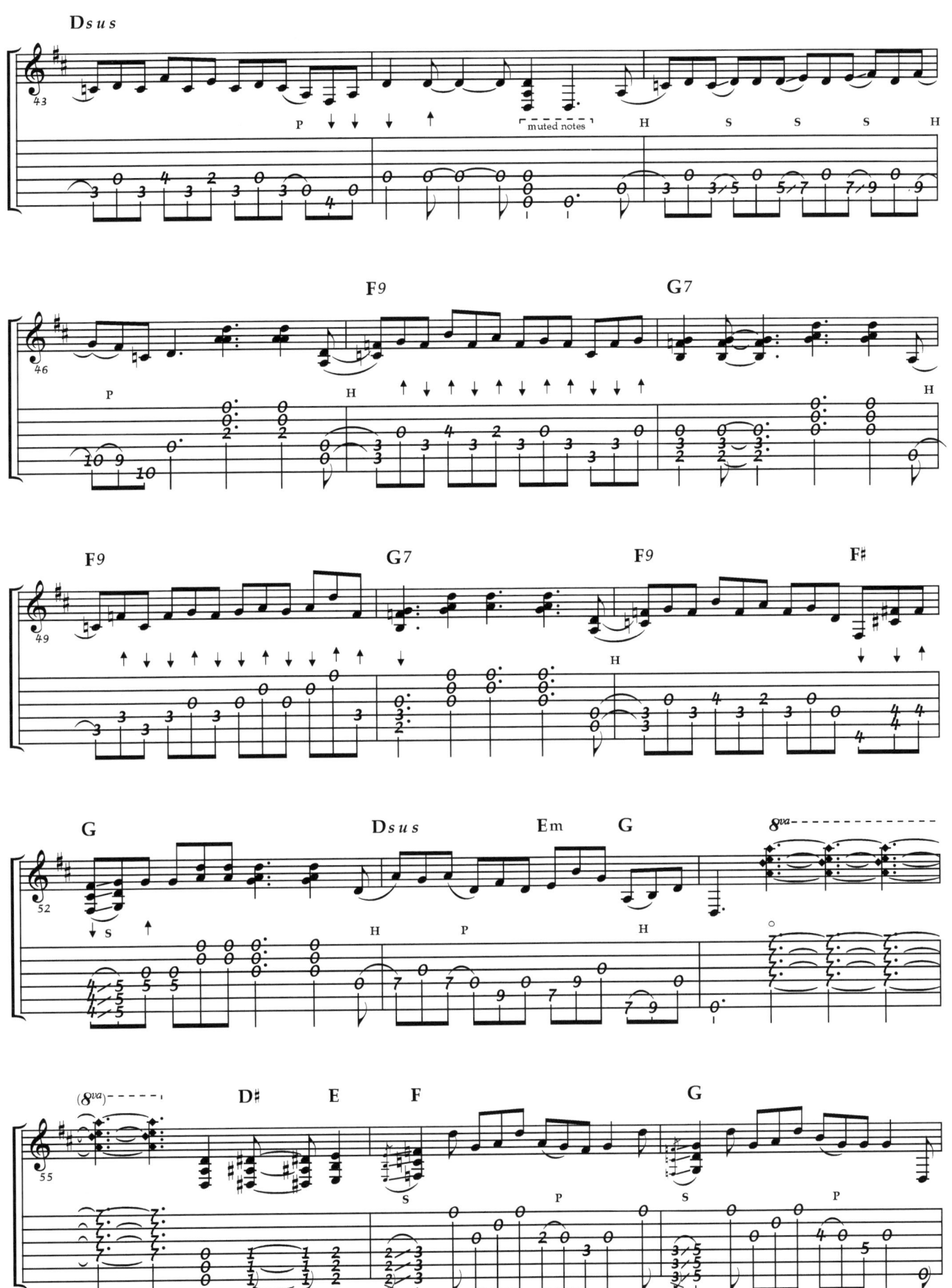

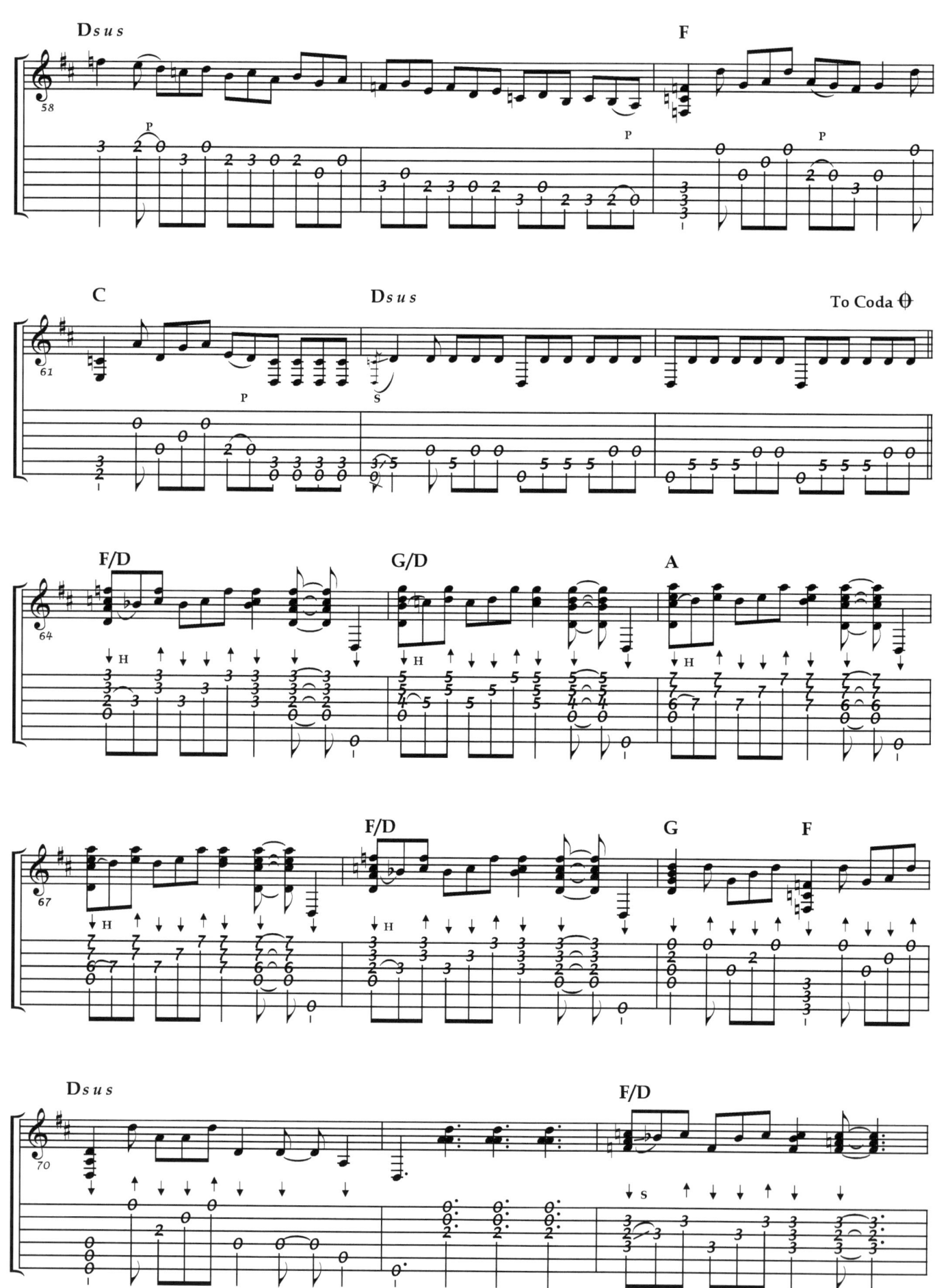

Fandango Per La Bionda

Music by Beppe Gambetta

Tuning: D A D G A D

Capo III

♩ = 167

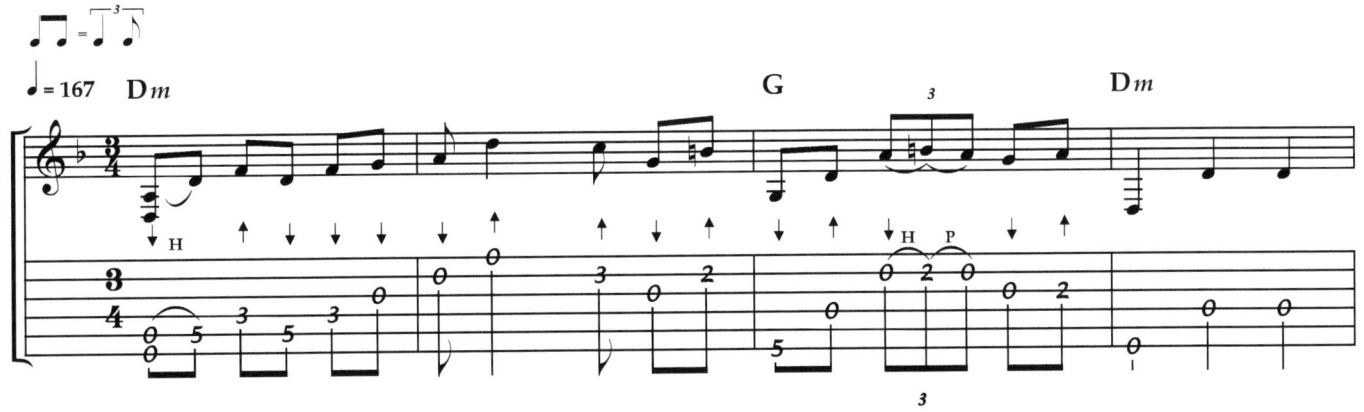

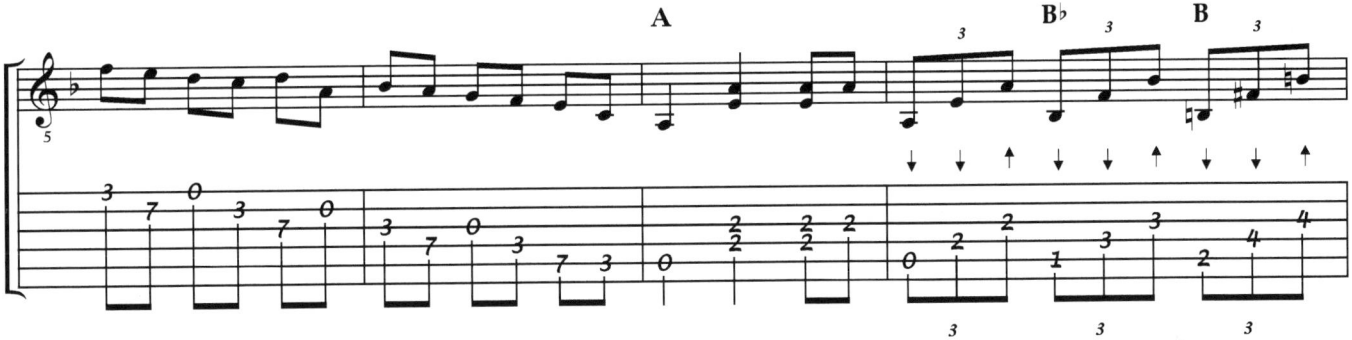

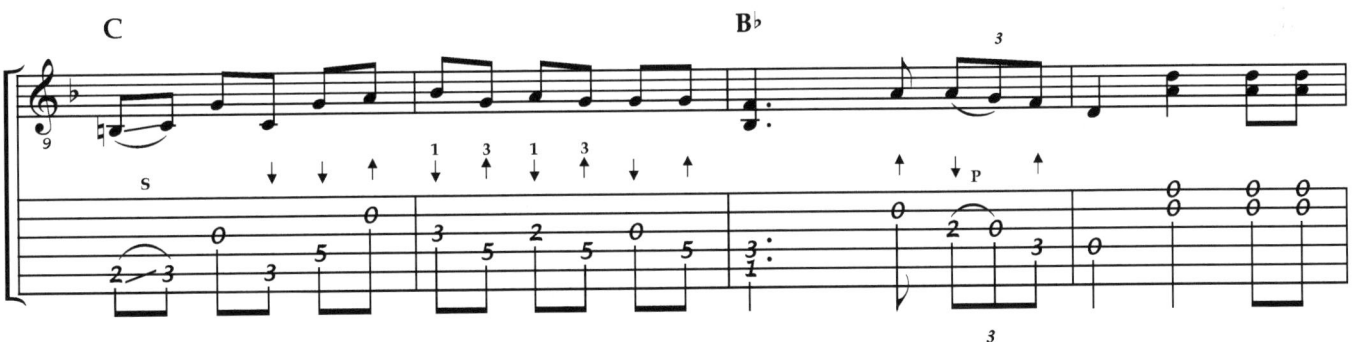

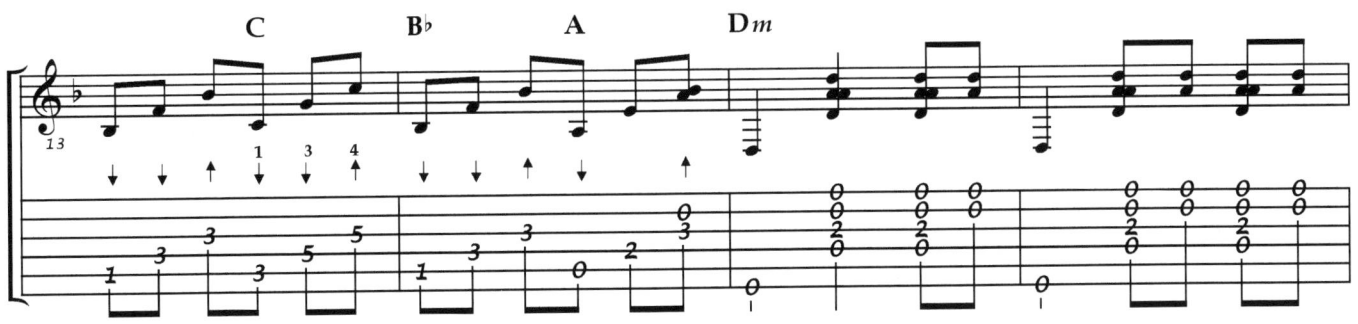

© 2002 Giuseppe Gambetta (SIAE - ITALY). All rights reserved. Used by permission.

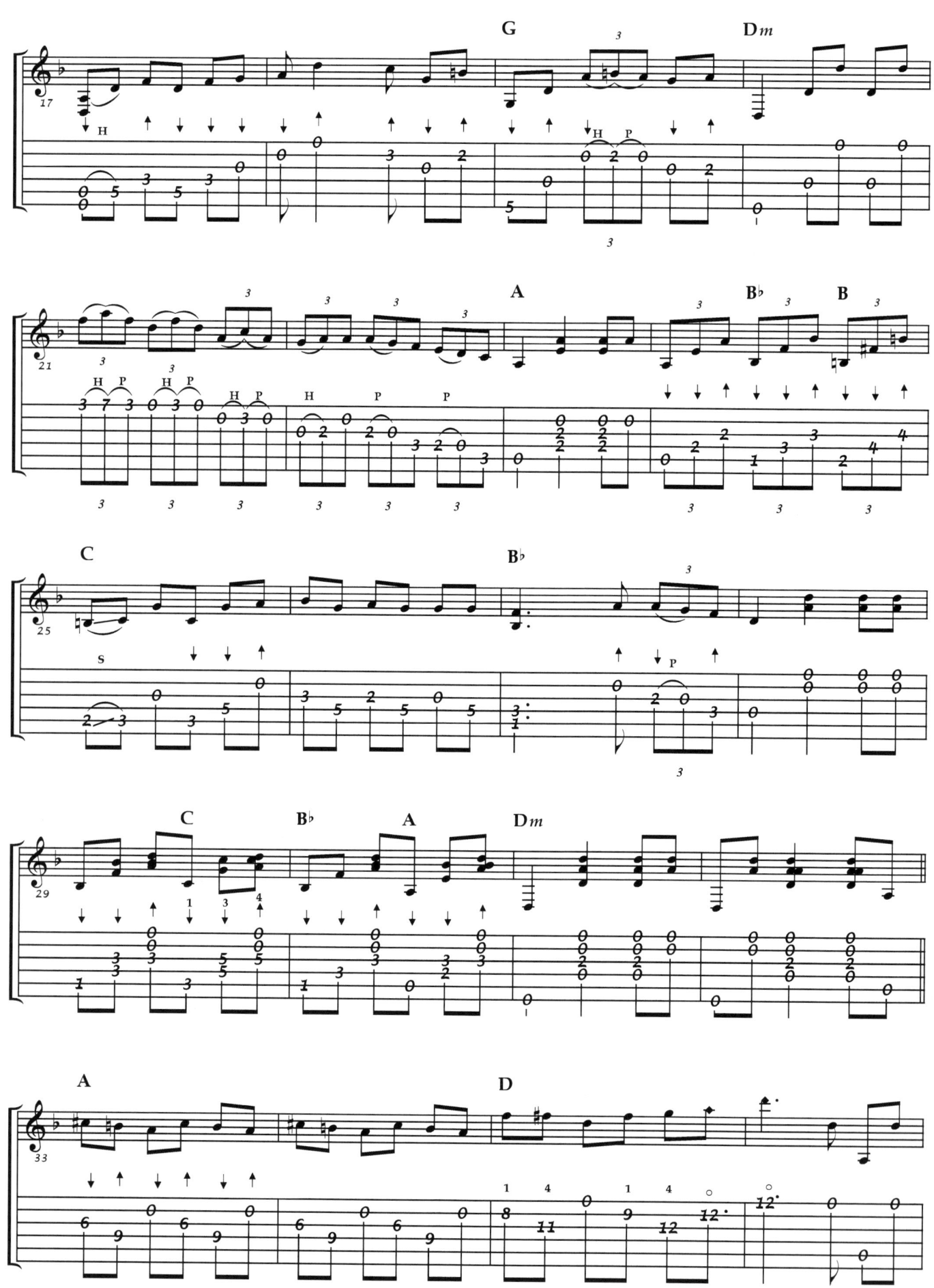

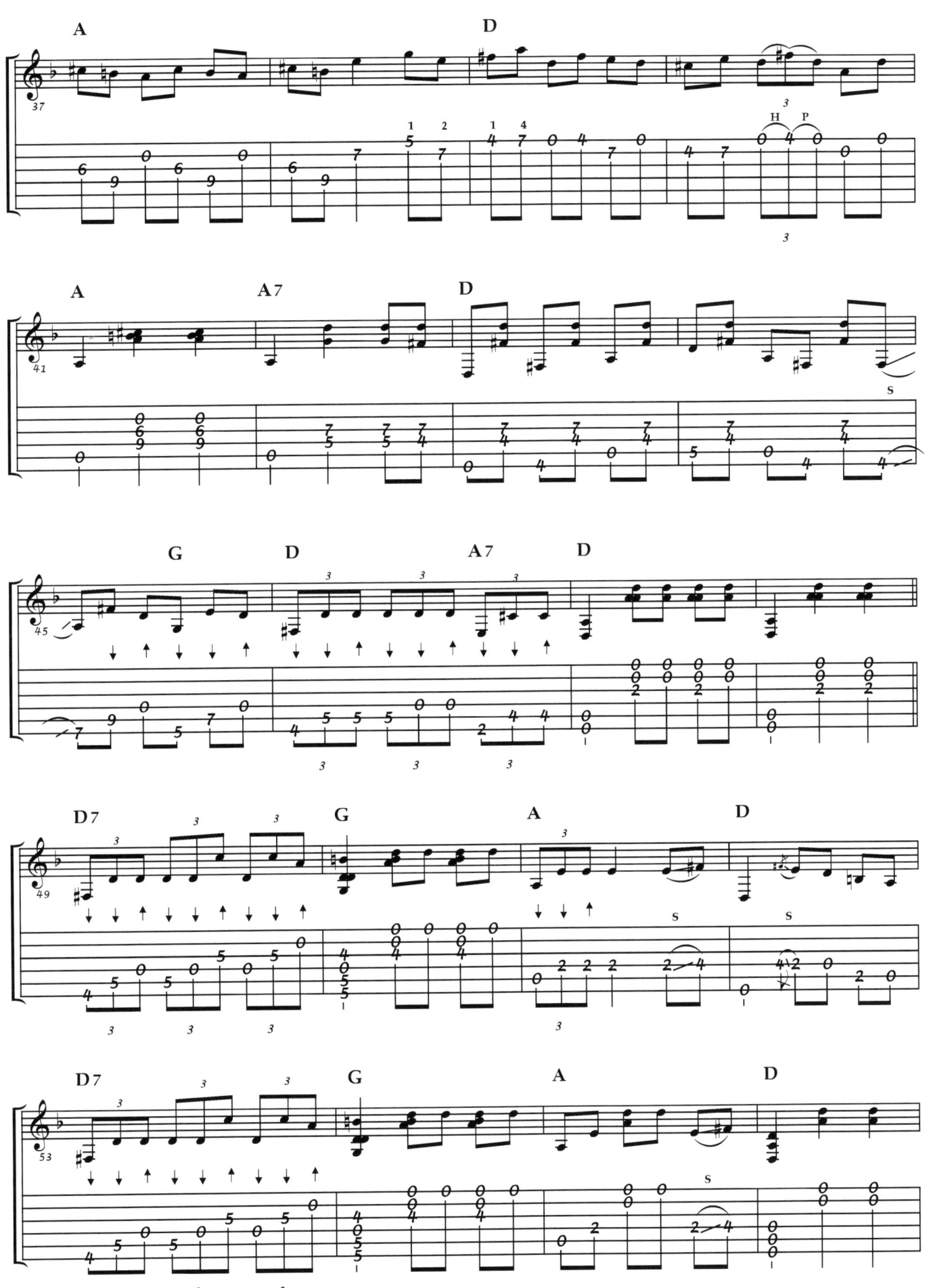

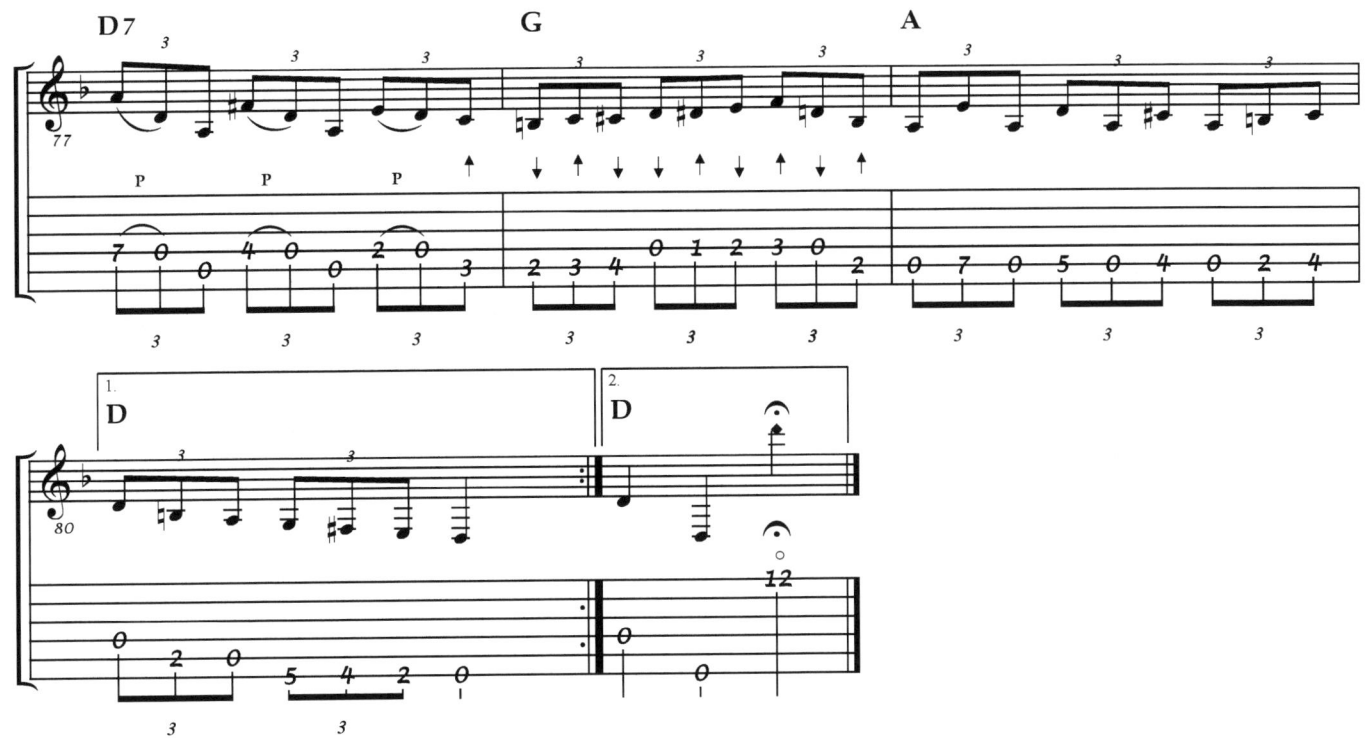

Church Street Blues

By Norman Blake, arranged by Beppe Gambetta

© 1976 by Happy Valley Music (BMI), International Copyright Secured. All Rights Reserved. Used by Permission.

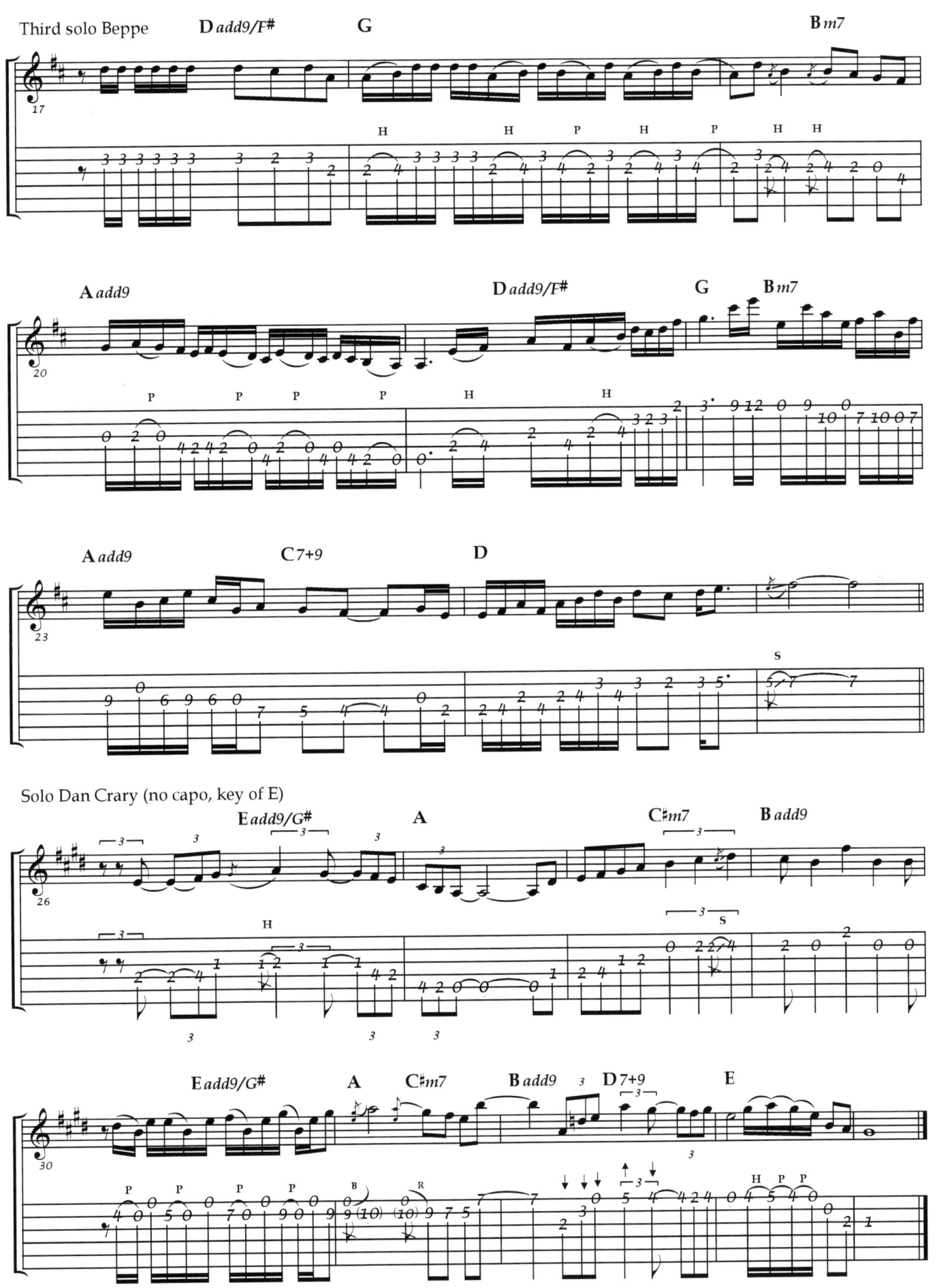

Church Street Blues

By Norman Blake, arranged by Beppe Gambetta

Capo II   Chord positions for the new vamp

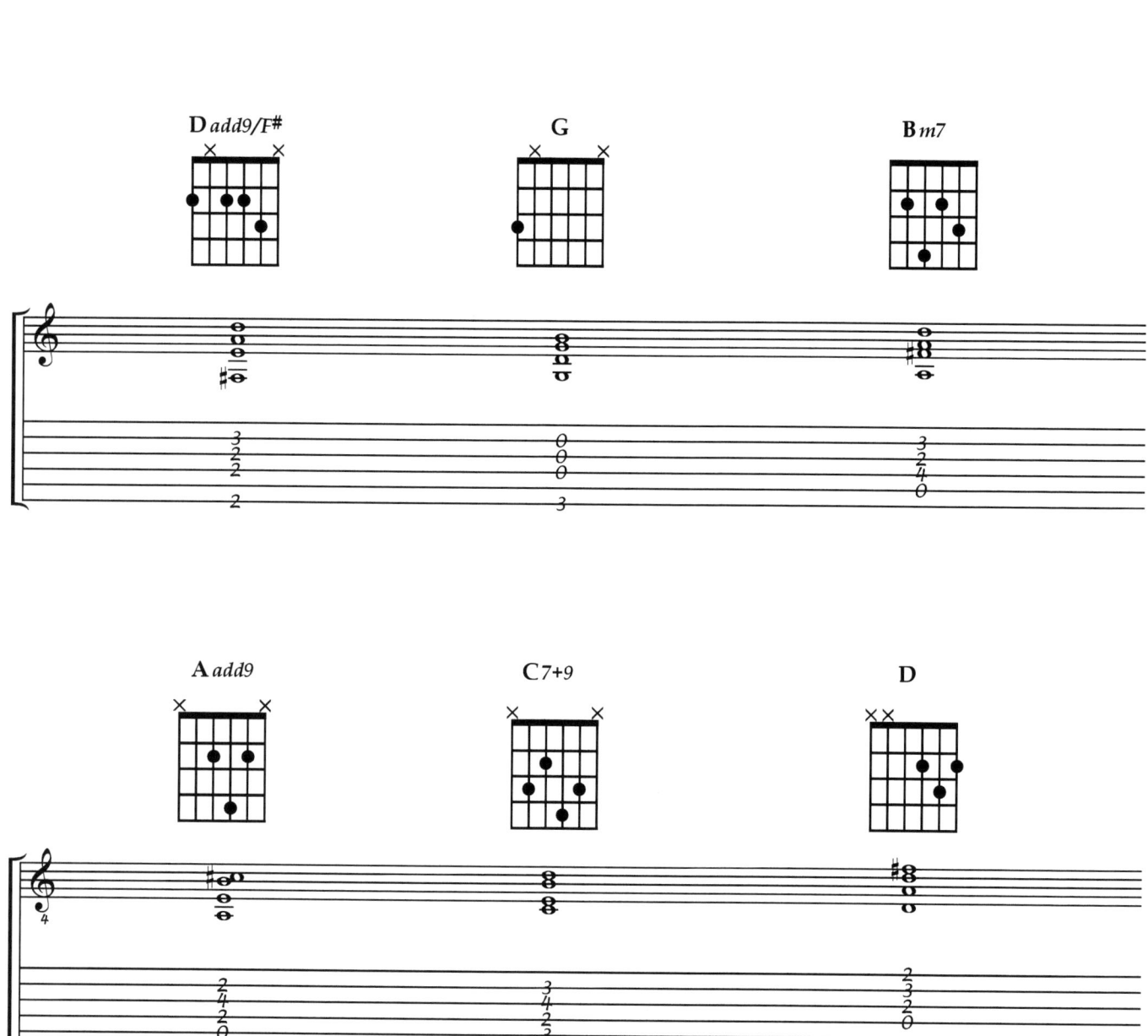

Chord progressions

Vamp

D D$_{add9/F\#}$ / G / G B$_{m7}$ / A$_{add9}$ / A$_{add9}$ D$_{add9/F\#}$ /
G B$_{m7}$ / A$_{add9}$ C$_{7+9}$ / D / D /

Verse

D / D$_{/G}$ / A$_{7sus4}$ / D / D / D$_{/G}$ / A$_{7sus4}$ / D /
D / D$_{/G}$ / A$_{7sus4}$ / D / D / D$_{/G}$ / A$_{7sus4}$ / D G /

Chorus

D D$_{add9/F\#}$ / G / G B$_{m7}$ / A$_{add9}$ / G A /
D / G G$_{/F\#}$ / Em A / G C$_{7+9}$ / D / D /

Shenandoah Valley Breakdown

Music by Kay Adelman & Buck Ryan, arranged by Beppe Gambetta

Tuning: D A D G A D

Capo V

First solo of Beppe

© Eagle Music Company., International Copyright Secured. All Rights Reserved. Used by Permission.

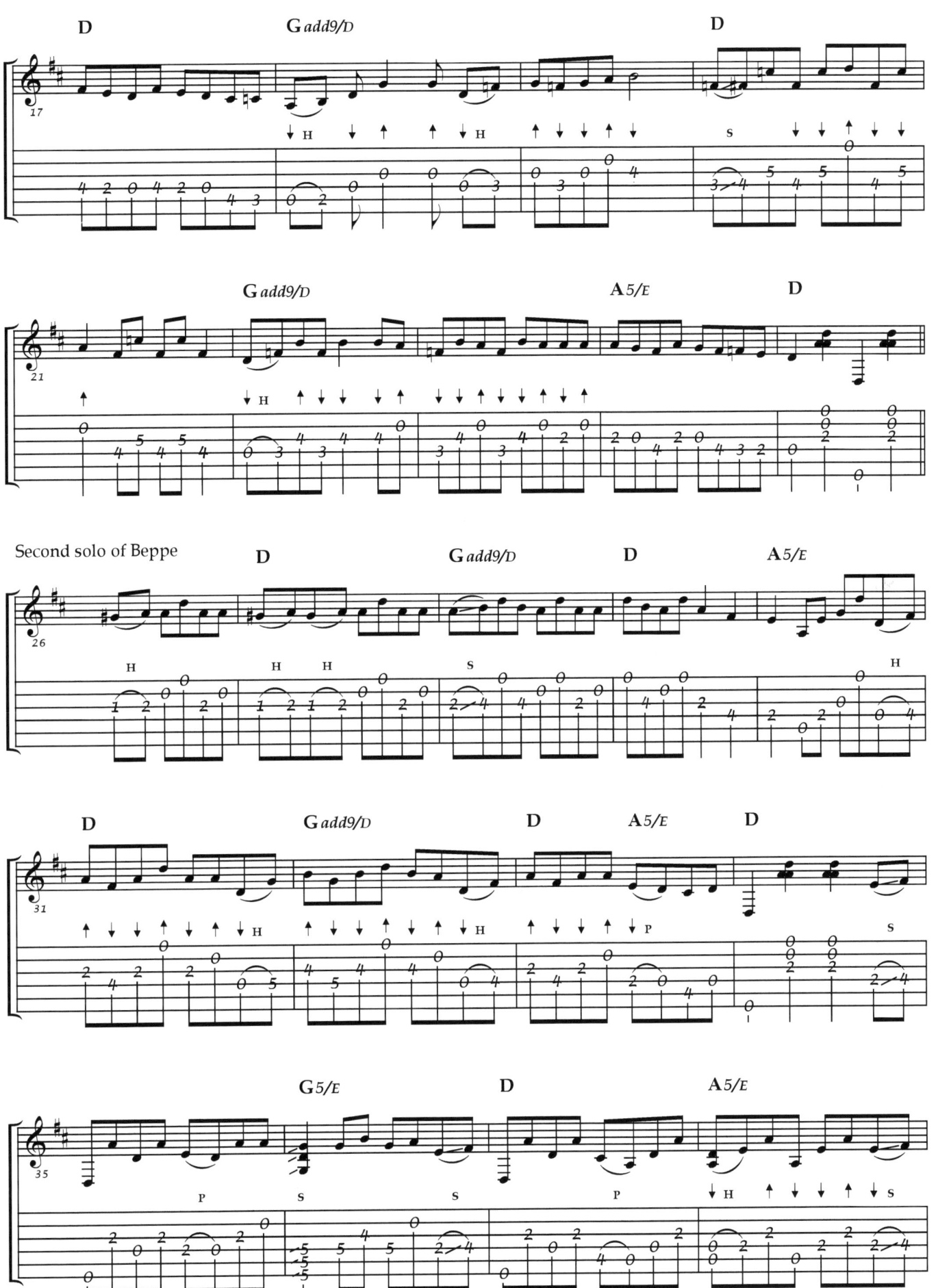

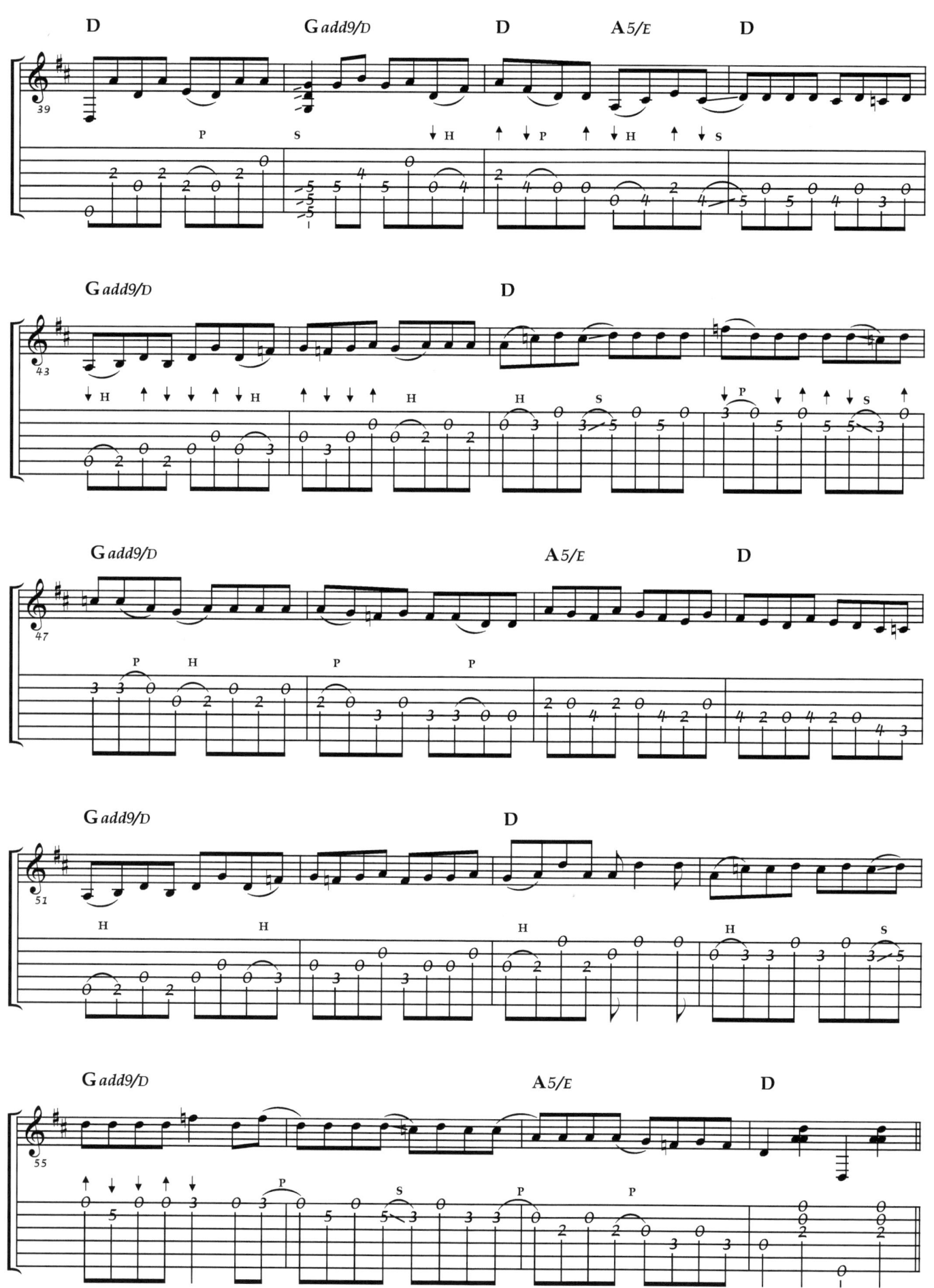

Final harmony part of Beppe (melody)

First solo of Dan
(standard tuning, no capo)

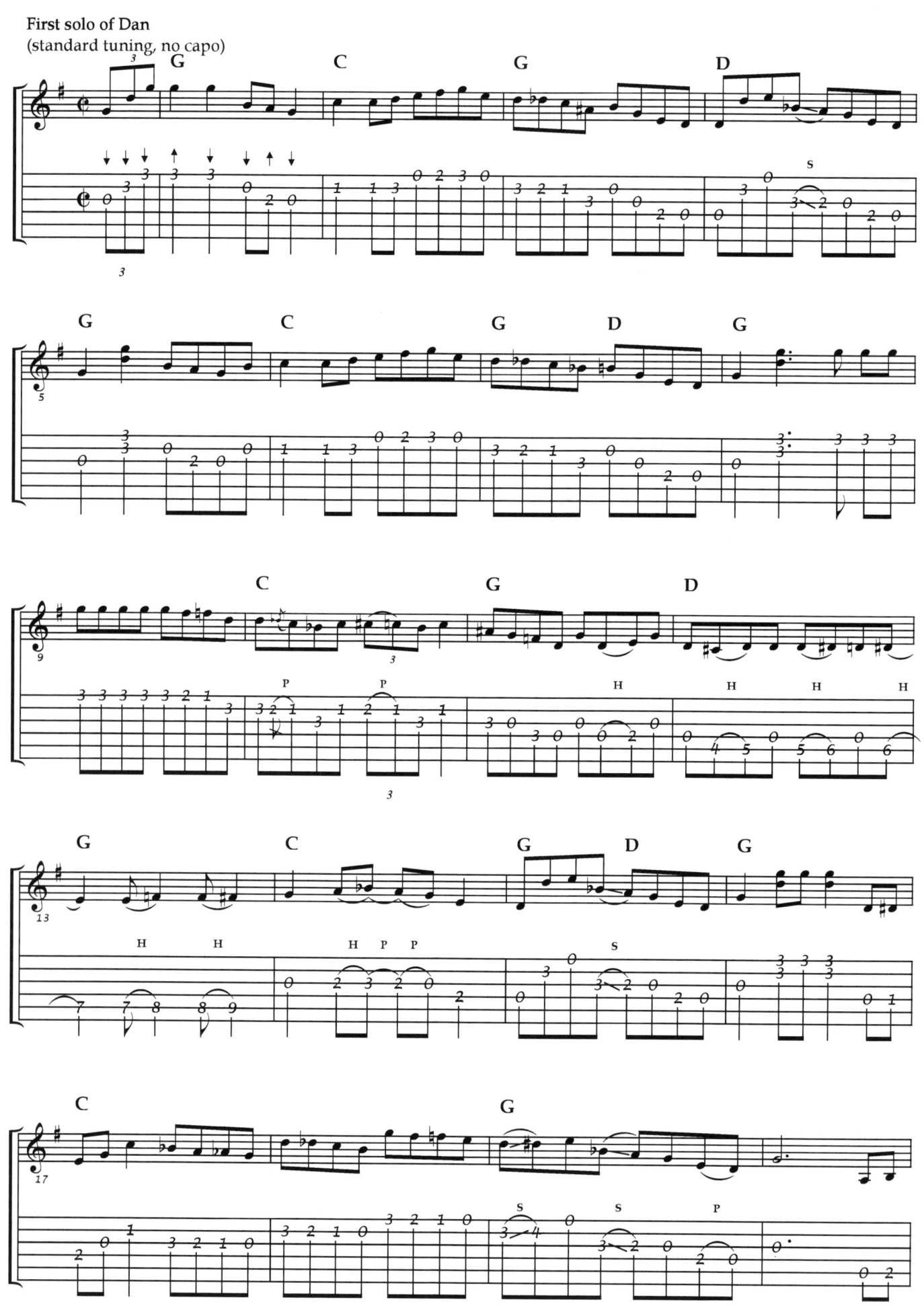

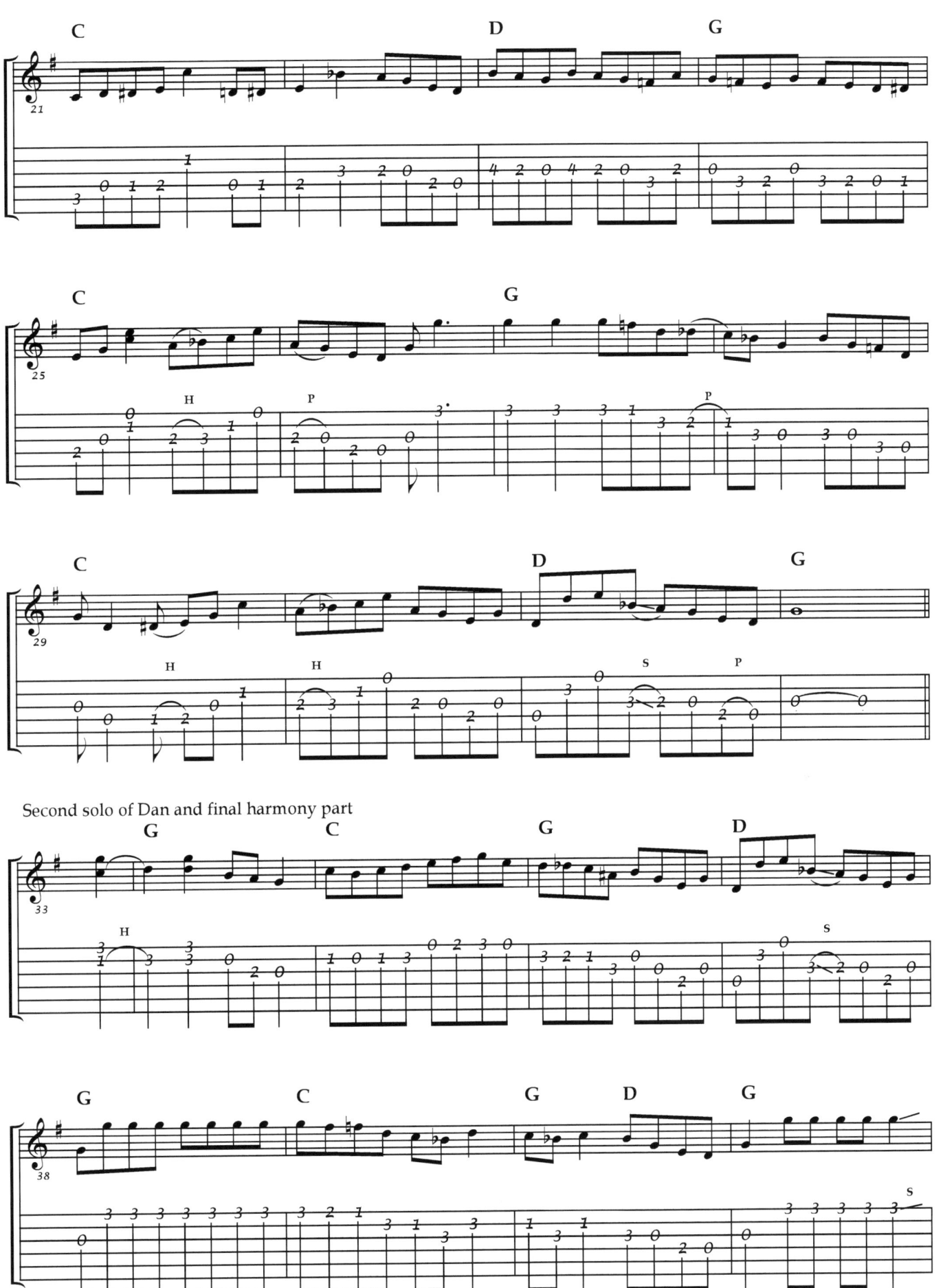

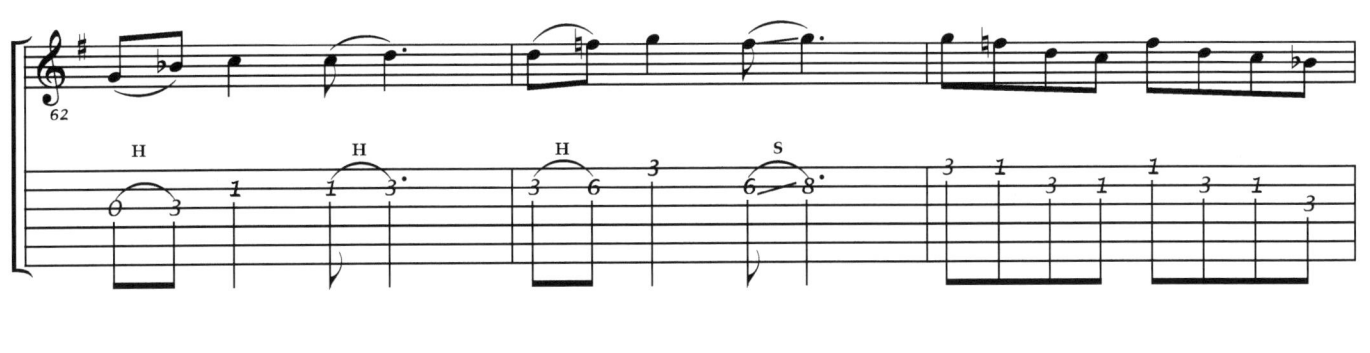

A Cimma

By Fabrizio De André / Ivano Fossati

Tuning: D A D E A E

Capo II

Chord positions to accompany the song

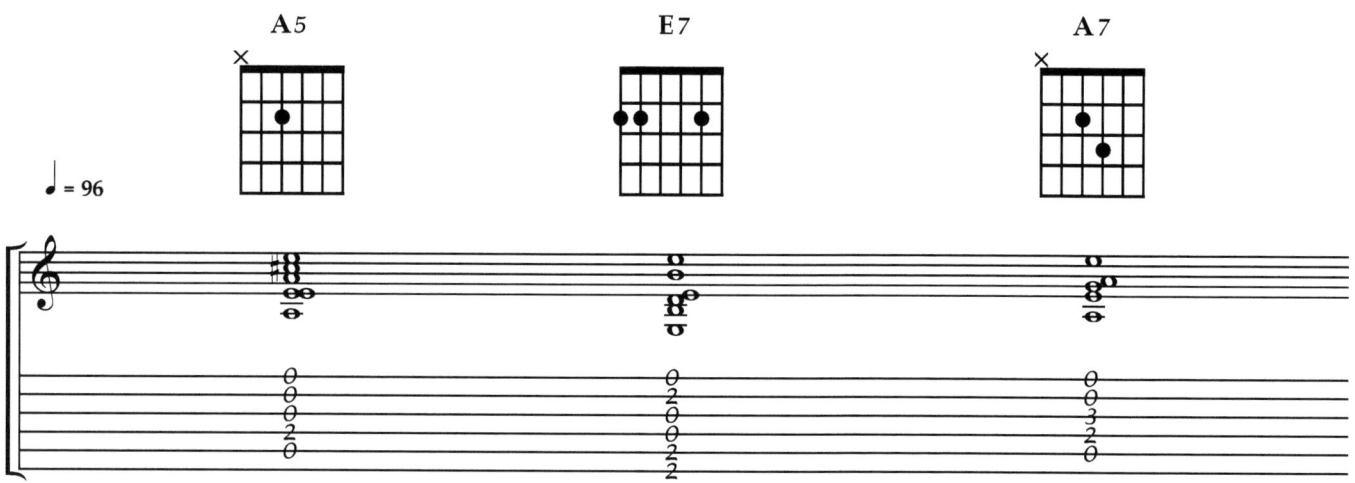

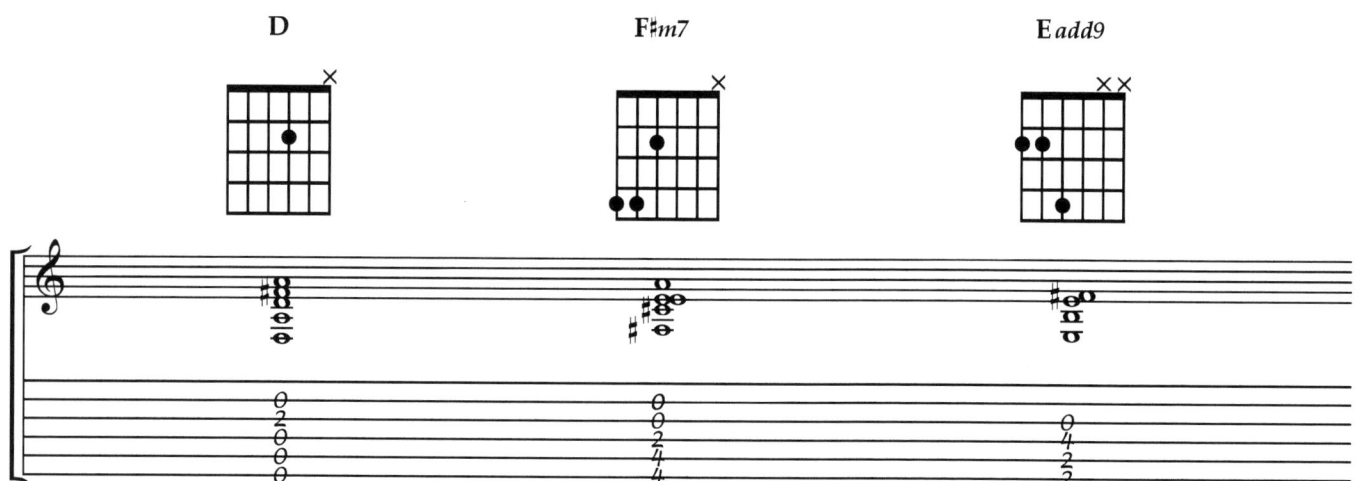

Chord progressions

Verse

A_5 / E_7 / A_5 / A_5 / A_5 / E_7 / A_5 / A_7 /
D / E_{add9} / A_5 / A_5 / E_7 / E_7 / A_5 / A_5 /
A_5 / E_7 / A_5 / A_5 / A_5 / E_7 / A_5 / A_7 /
D / E_{add9} / A_5 / A_5 / E_7 / E_7 / A_5 / A_7 /

Chorus

D / E_{add9} / A_5 / $F\#m_7$ / D / E_{add9} / A_5 / $F\#m_7$ /
D / E_{add9} / A_5 / $F\#m_7$ / D / E_{add9} / A_5 / A_5 /

Instrumental part

E_7 / E_7 / D A / D A / E_7 / E_7 / D A / D A /
E_7 / E_7 / D A / D / D / D / D /

Sestrina

Traditional Italian dance, arranged by Beppe Gambetta

Tuning: D A D E A E

Capo II

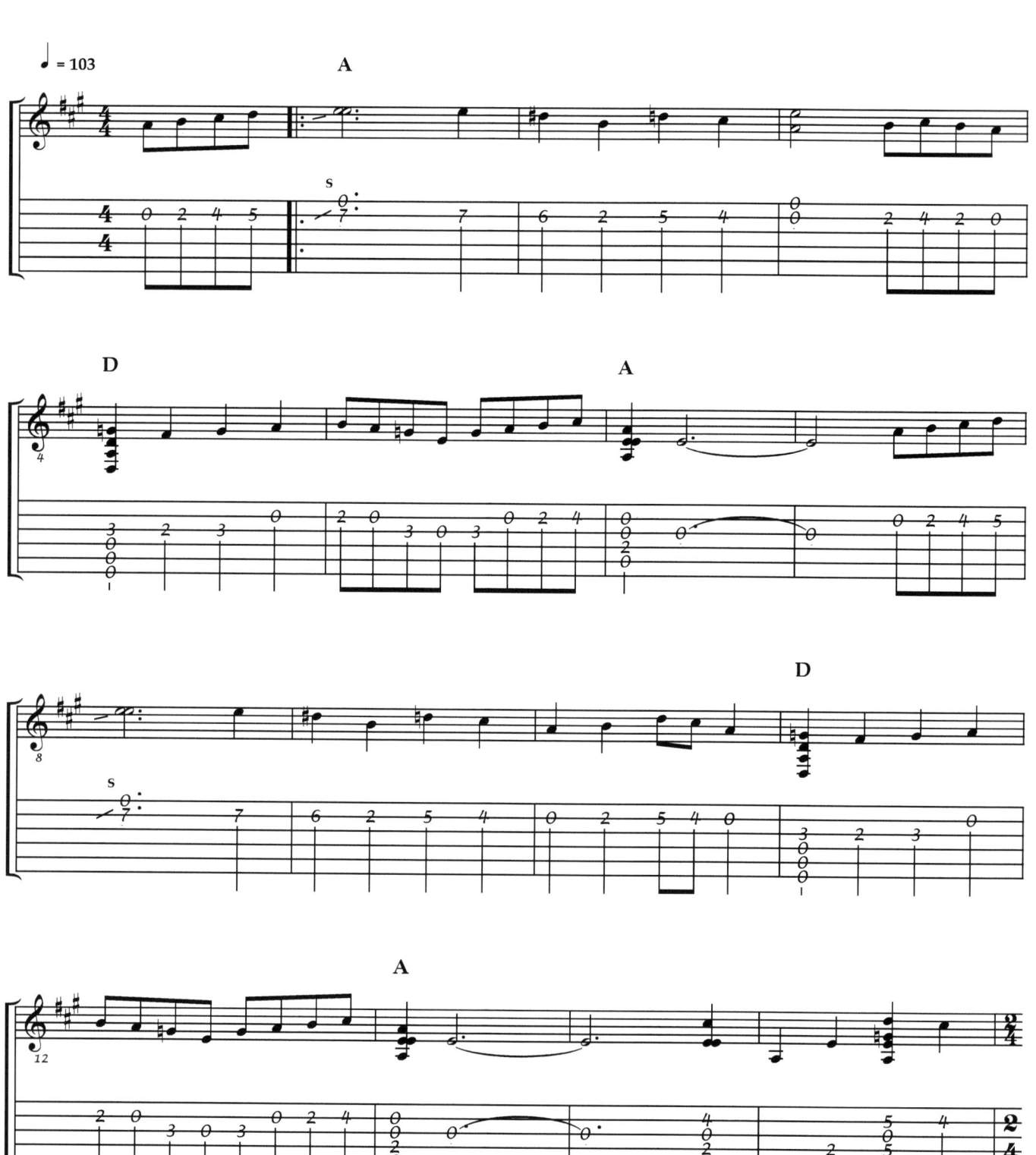

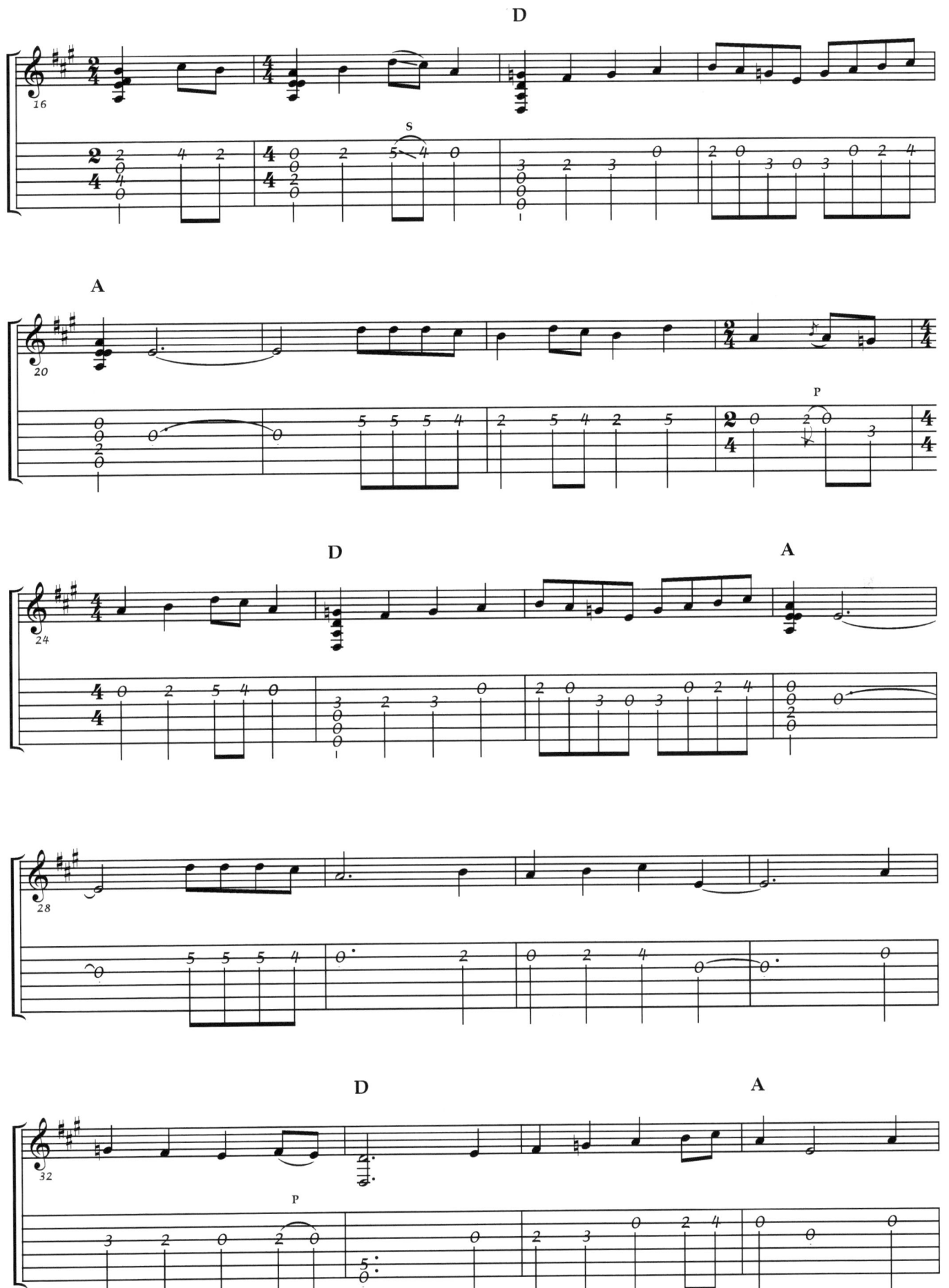

Sestrina

Traditional Italian dance, arranged by Beppe Gambetta
Rearranged version for solo flatpicking guitar

Tuning: D A D E A E

Capo II

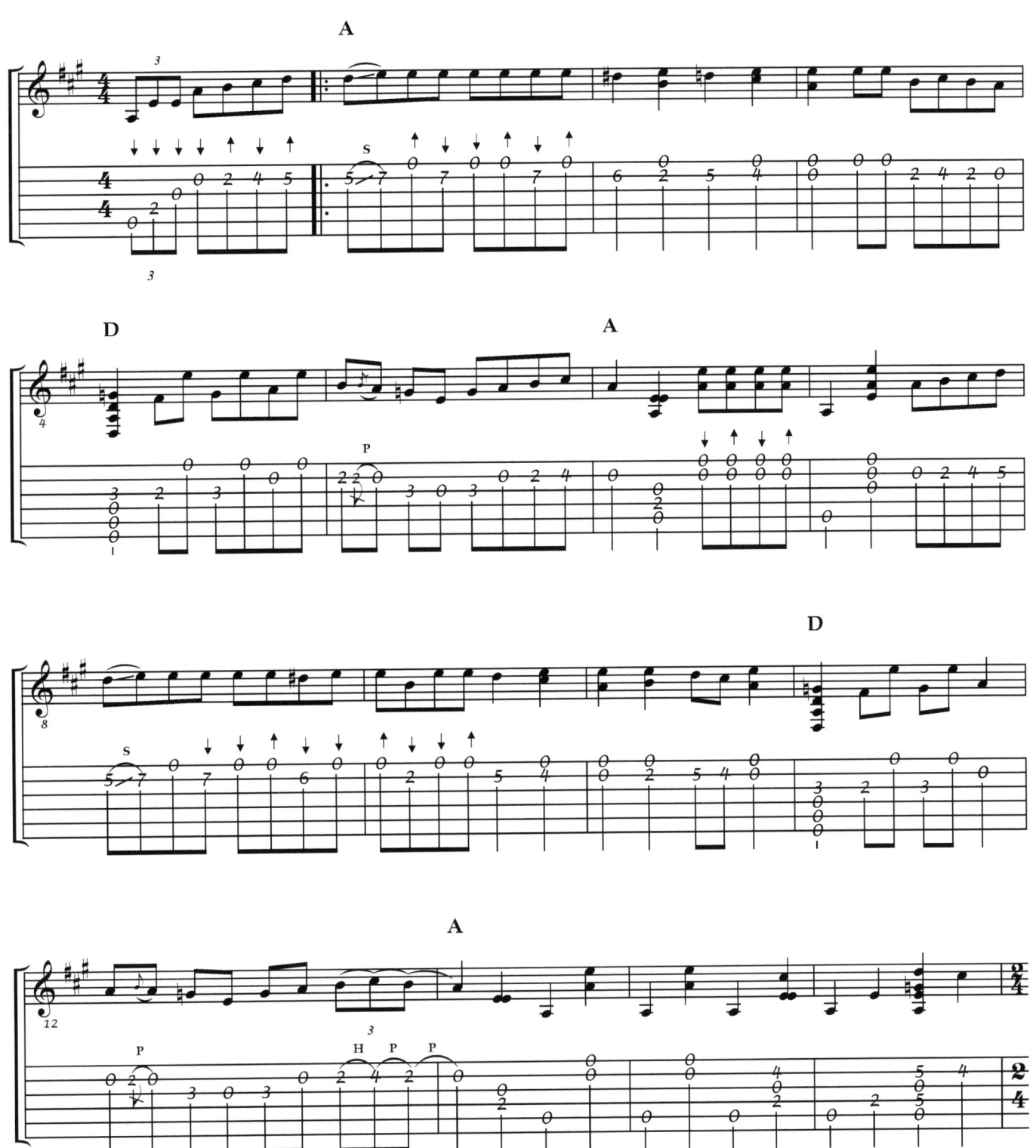

© 2002 Giuseppe Gambetta (SIAE - ITALY). All rights reserved. Used by permission.

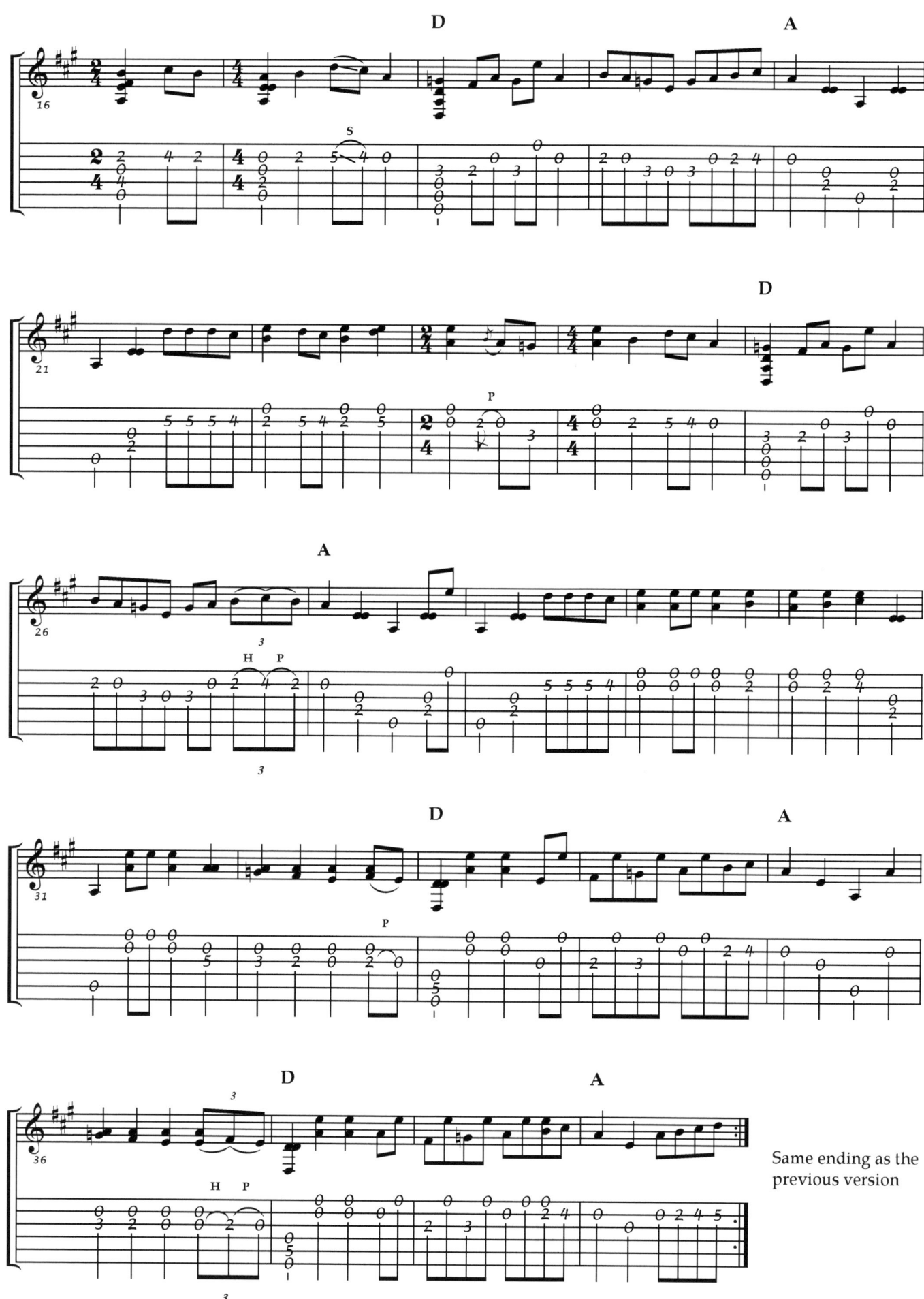

A Night in Frontenac

Music by Beppe Gambetta

Tuning: D A D G A D

Capo II

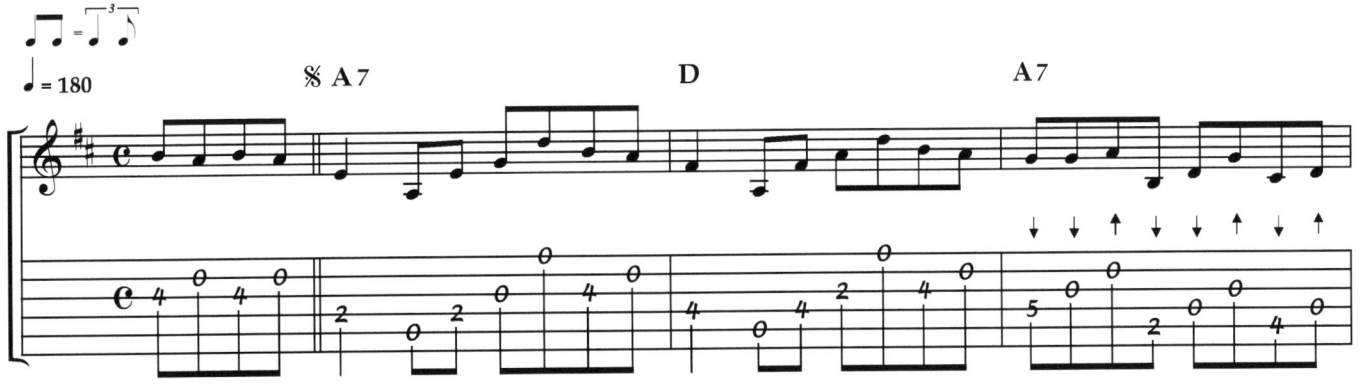

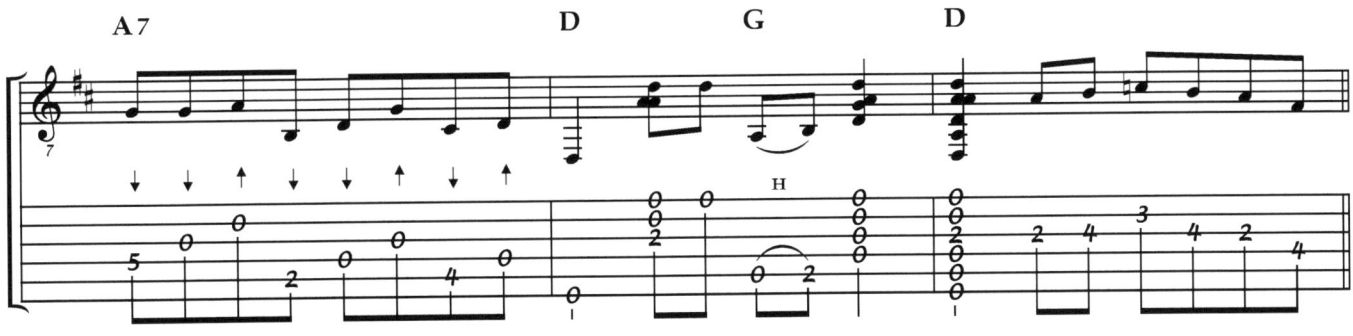
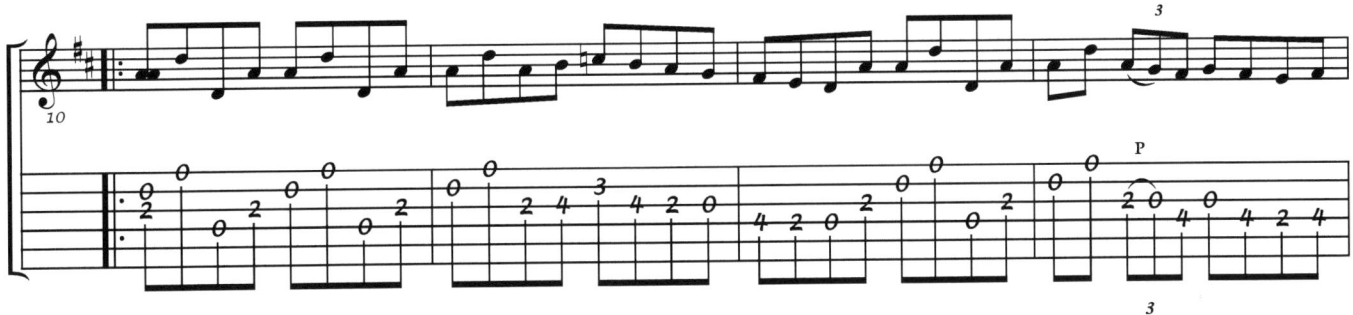

© 2002 Giuseppe Gambetta (SIAE - ITALY). All rights reserved. Used by permission.

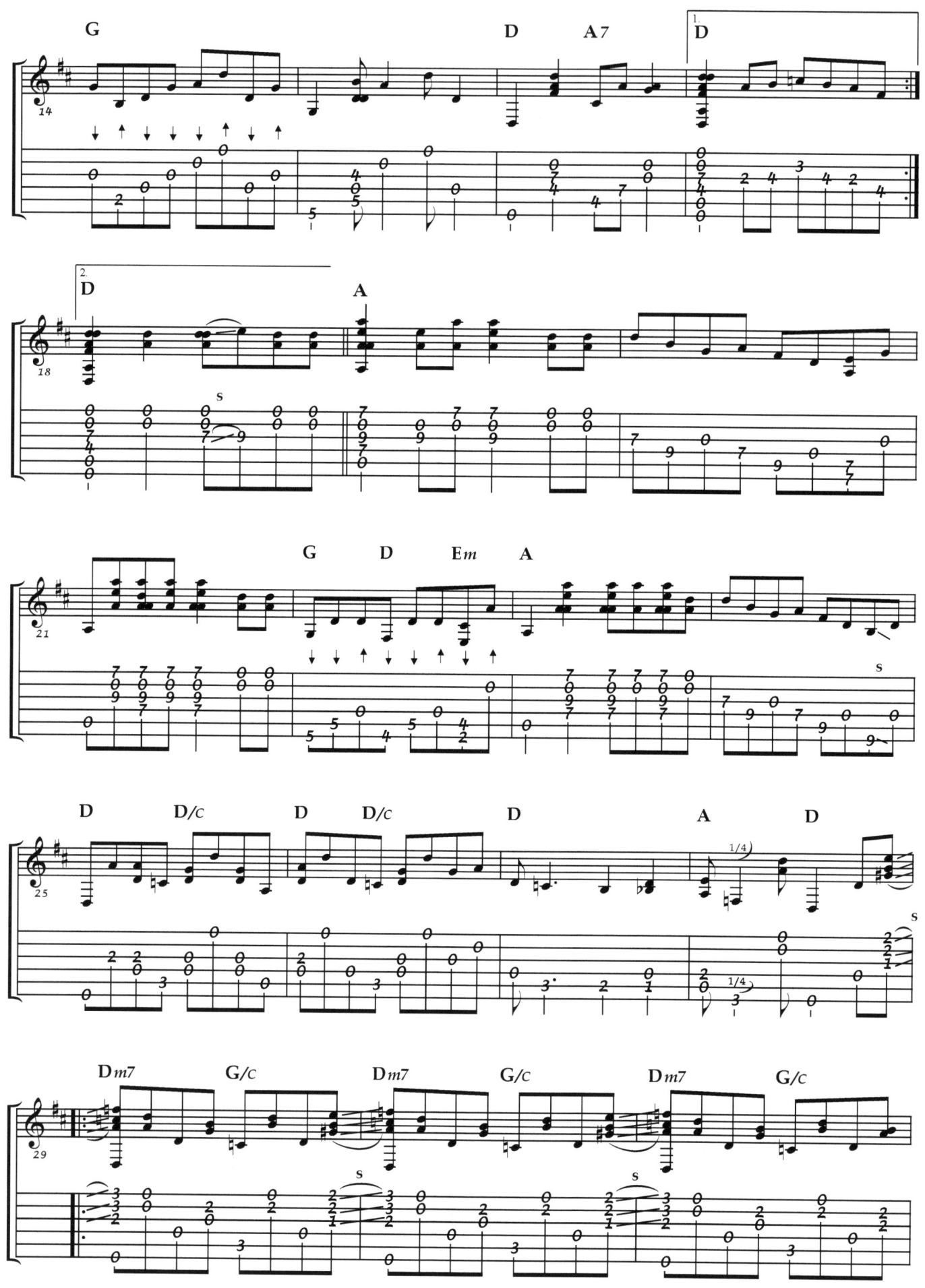

Nova Gelosia

Anonimo, arranged by Beppe Gambetta

Tuning: D G D G A D

Capo III

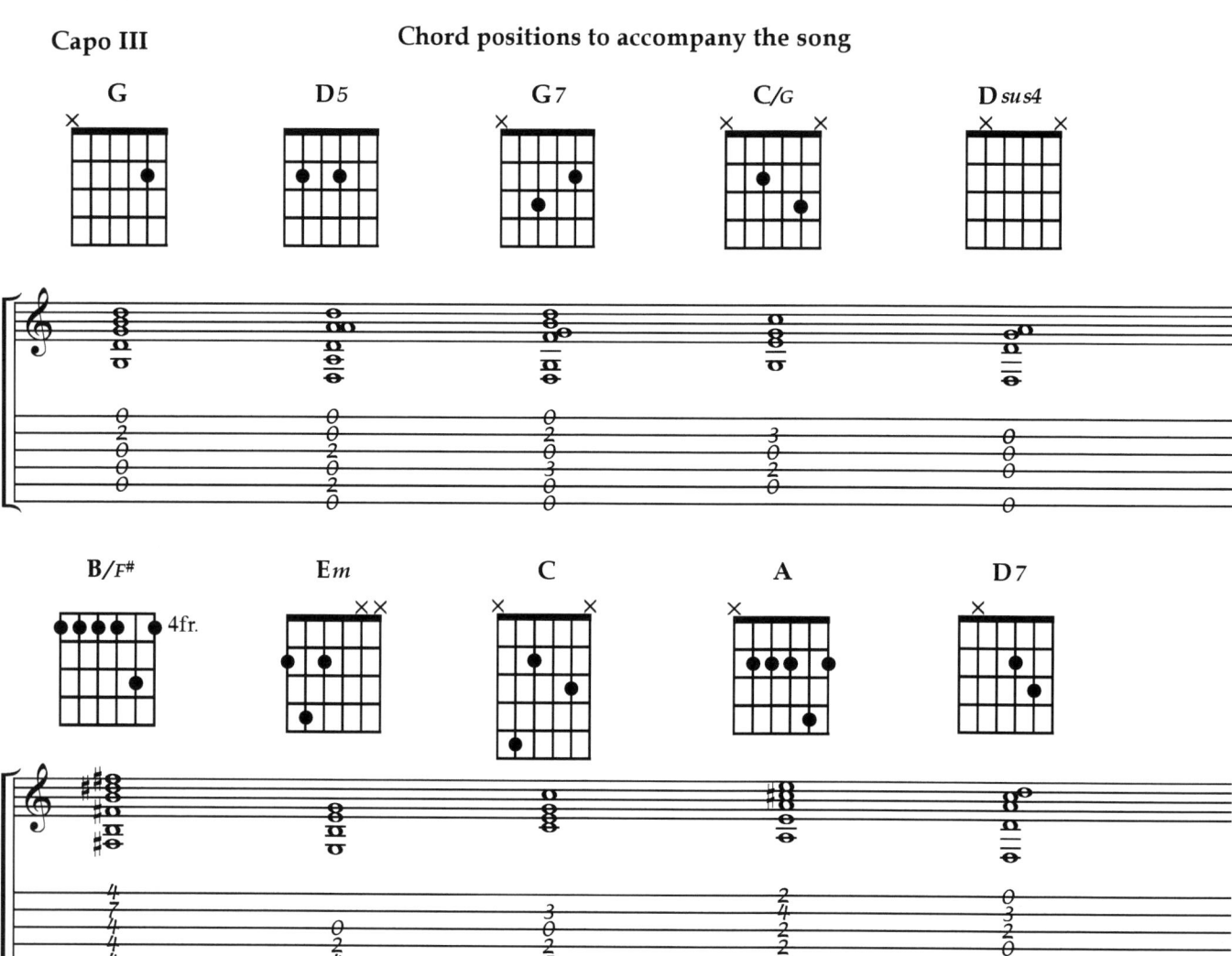

Chord Progressions

First Verse

G / D5 / G / G / G7 / C/G / Dsus4 / D5 / G / B/F# / Em / C / G / A D7 / G / G /

Second Verse

D5 / D5 / G / G / D5 / D5 / G / G / G / B/F# / Em / C / G / A D7 / G / G /

© 2002 Giuseppe Gambetta (SIAE - ITALY). All rights reserved. Used by permission.

Serenata

Music by Beppe Gambetta

Tuning: D G D G A D

Capo III

© 2002 Giuseppe Gambetta (SIAE - ITALY). All rights reserved. Used by permission.

Tarantexas

Music by Beppe Gambetta

Tuning: D A D G A D

Intro

Freely

♩. = 146

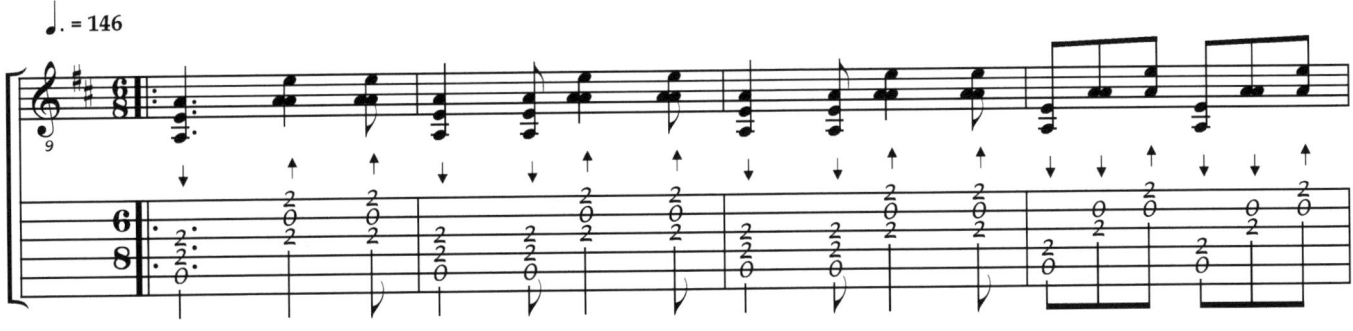

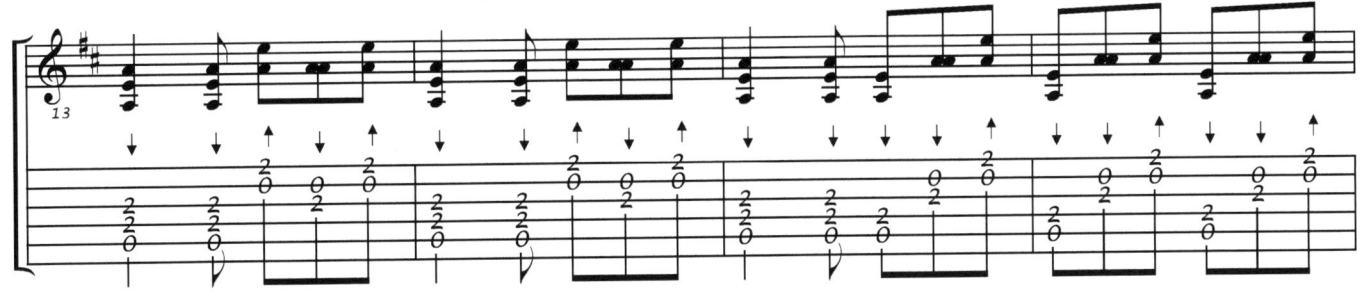

© 2002 Giuseppe Gambetta (SIAE - ITALY). All rights reserved. Used by permission.

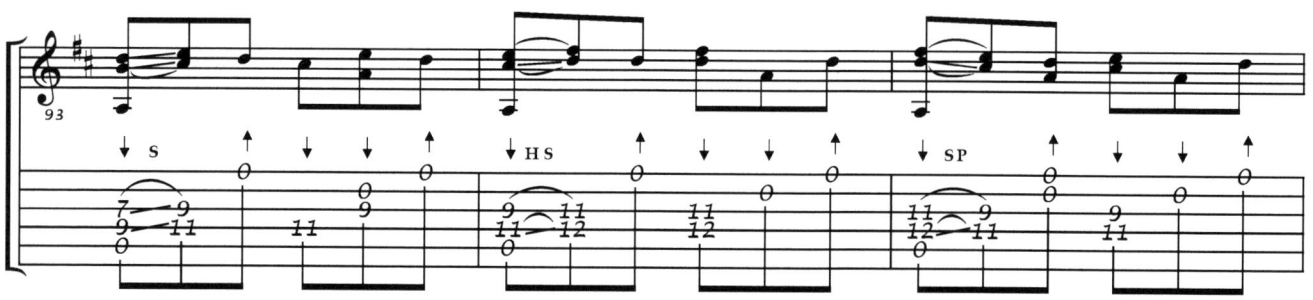

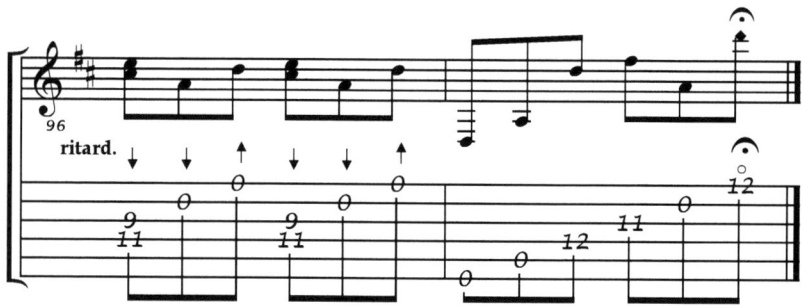

Fuinde

Music by Beppe Gambetta

Tuning: D G D G A D **Barking dog:** Bb

Capo III

Intro

Freely

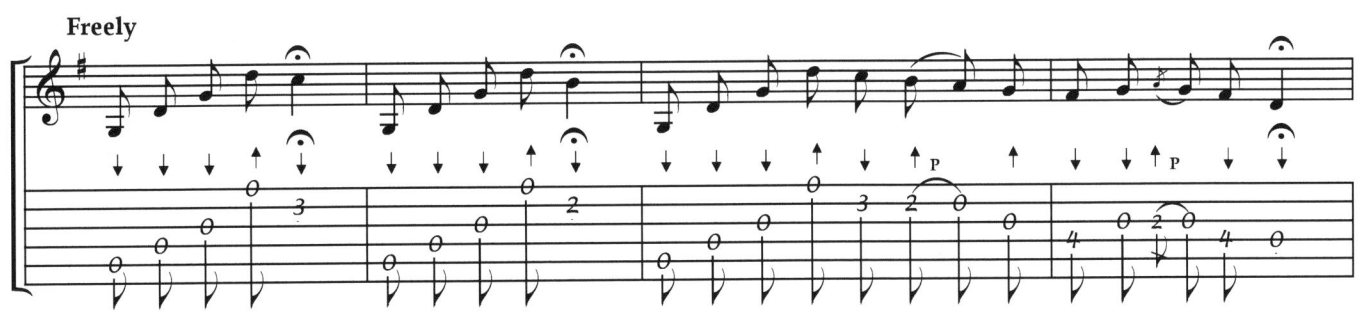

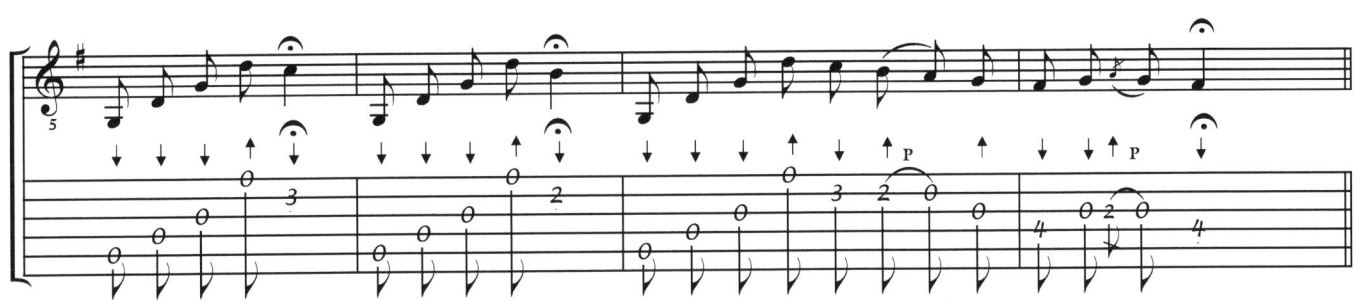

♩ = 170

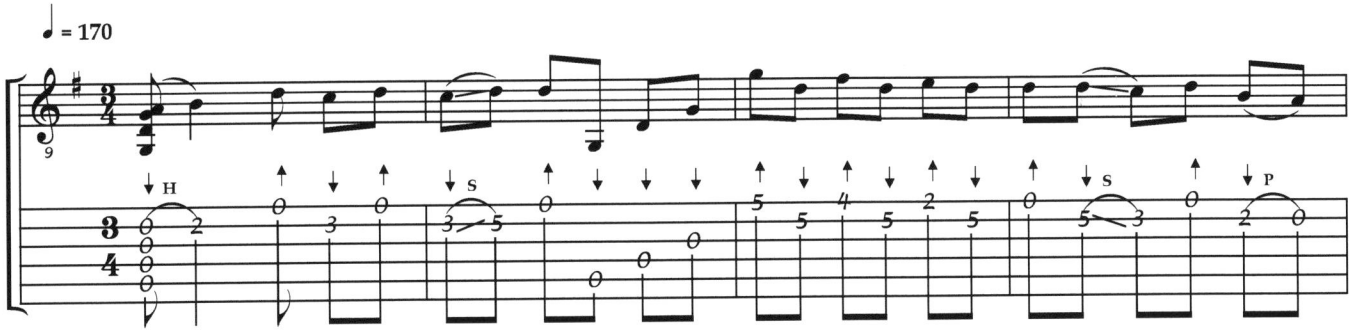

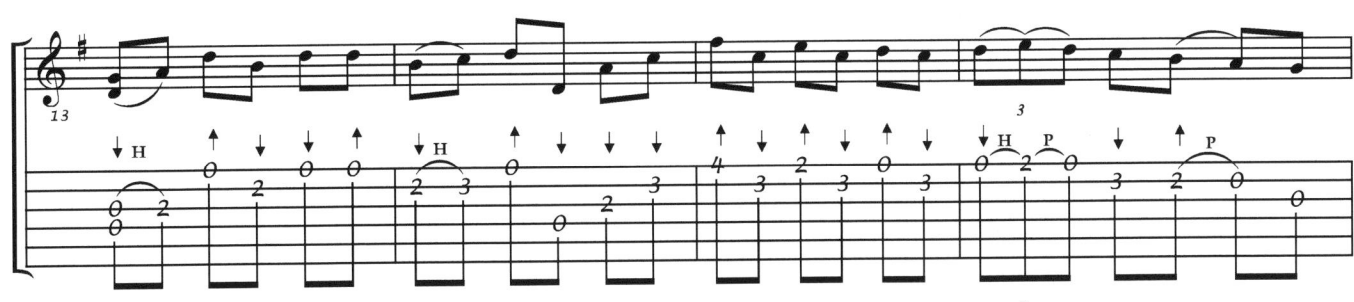

© 2002 Giuseppe Gambetta (SIAE - ITALY). All rights reserved. Used by permission.

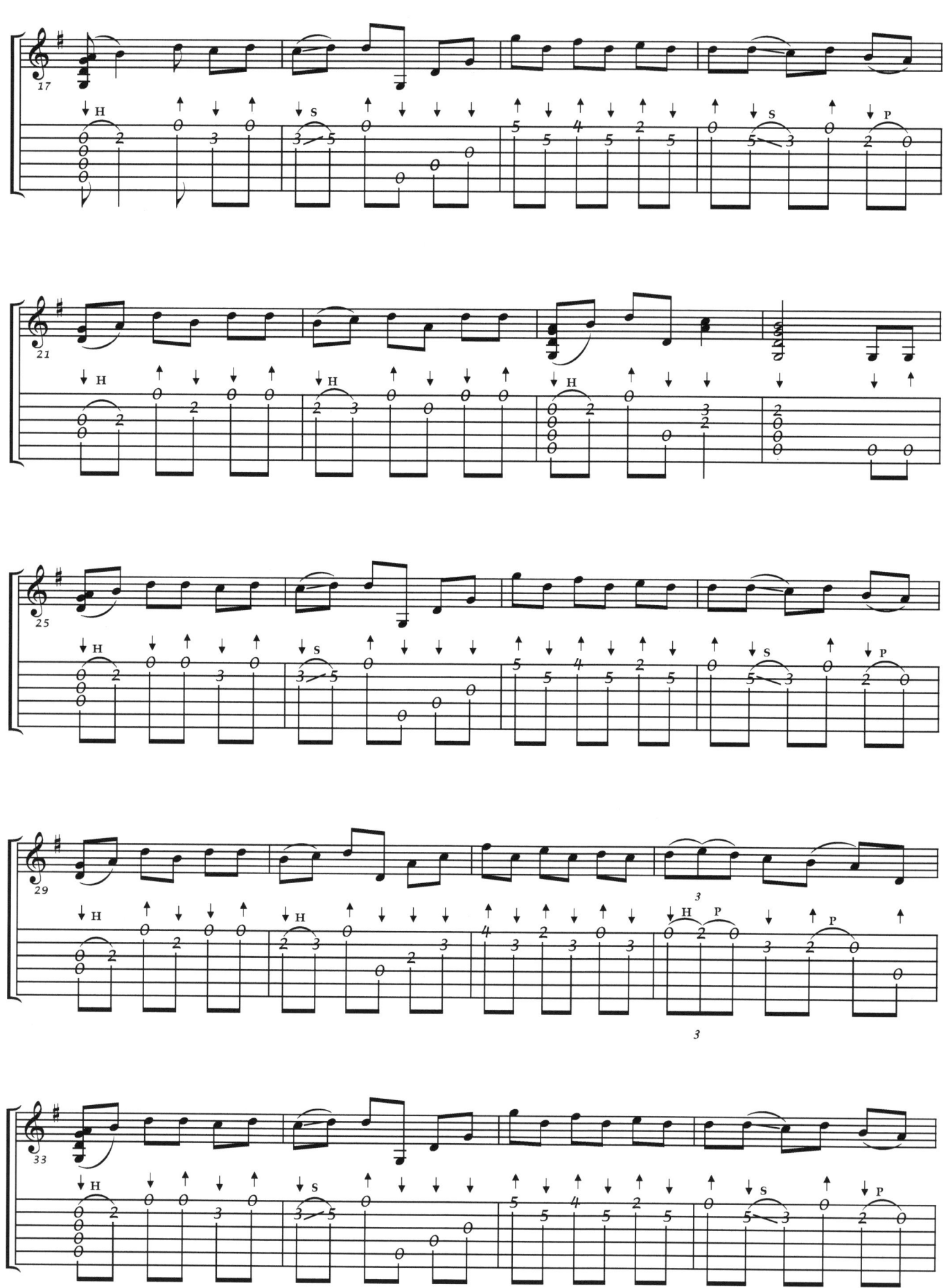

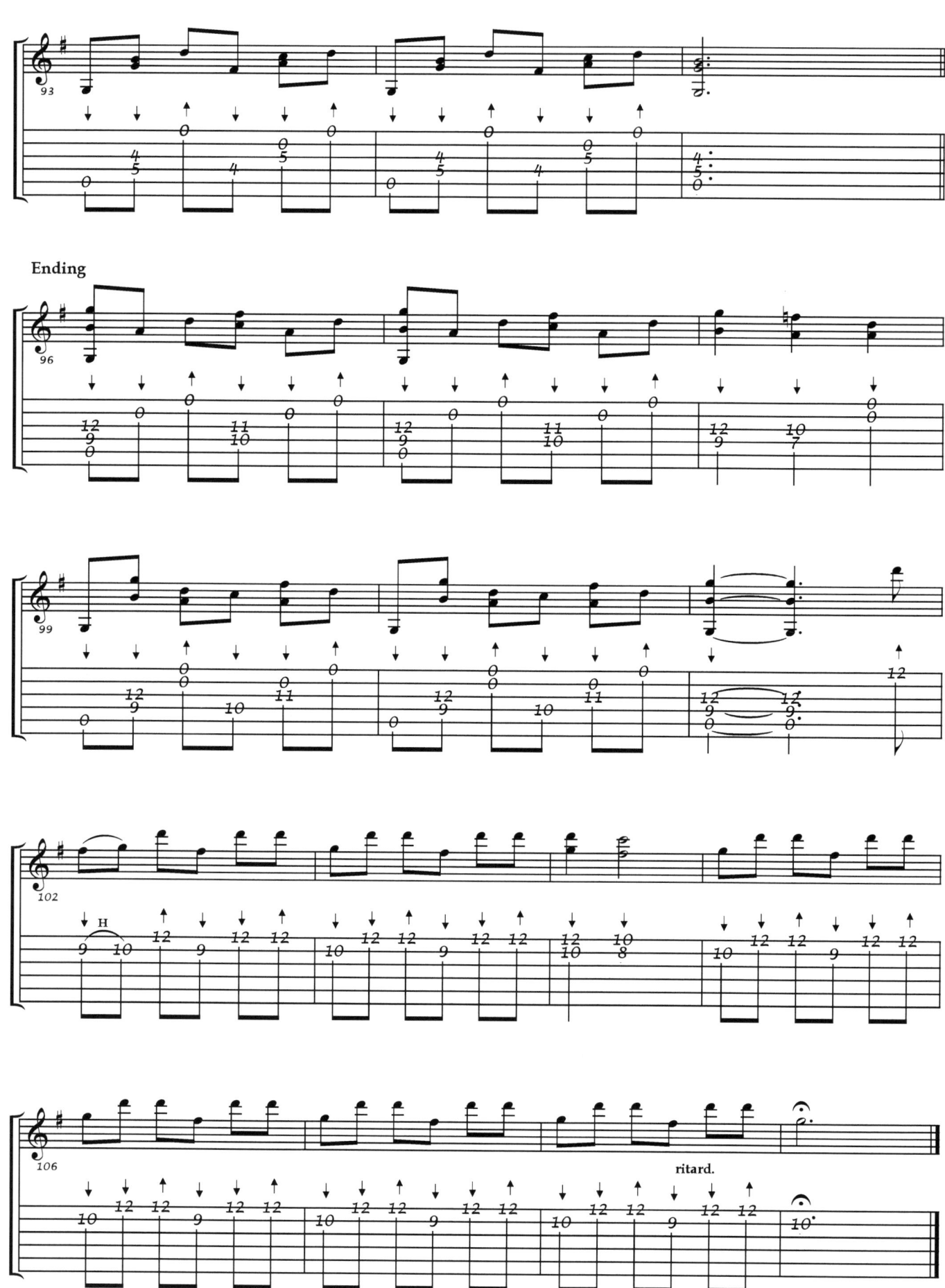

Ending

Main variation on the repetition

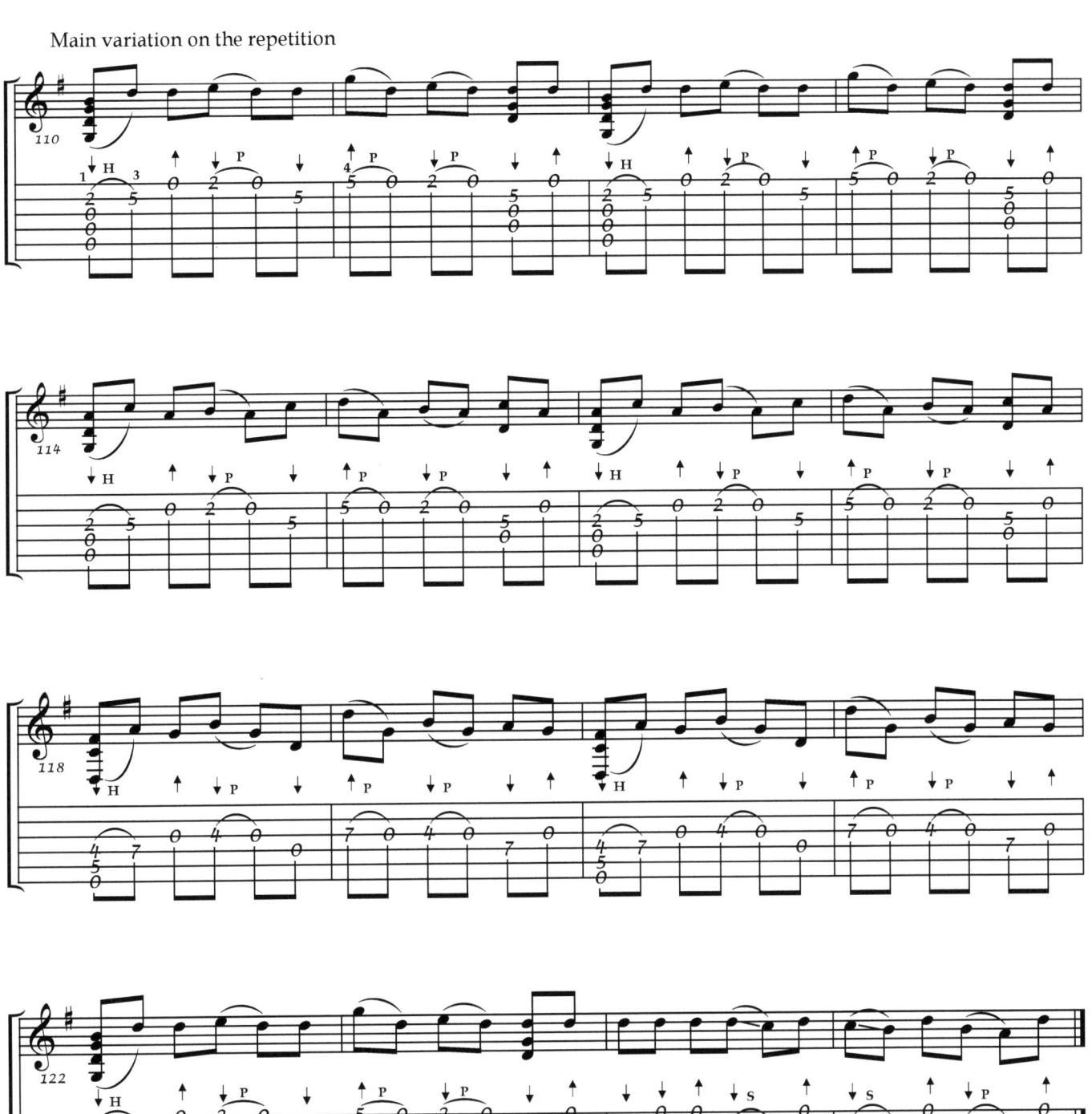

Marcia Americana

Music by Pasquale Taraffo (Genova 1887 - Buenos Aires 1937)
Arranged by Beppe Gambetta

© 2002 Giuseppe Gambetta (SIAE - ITALY). All rights reserved. Used by permission.

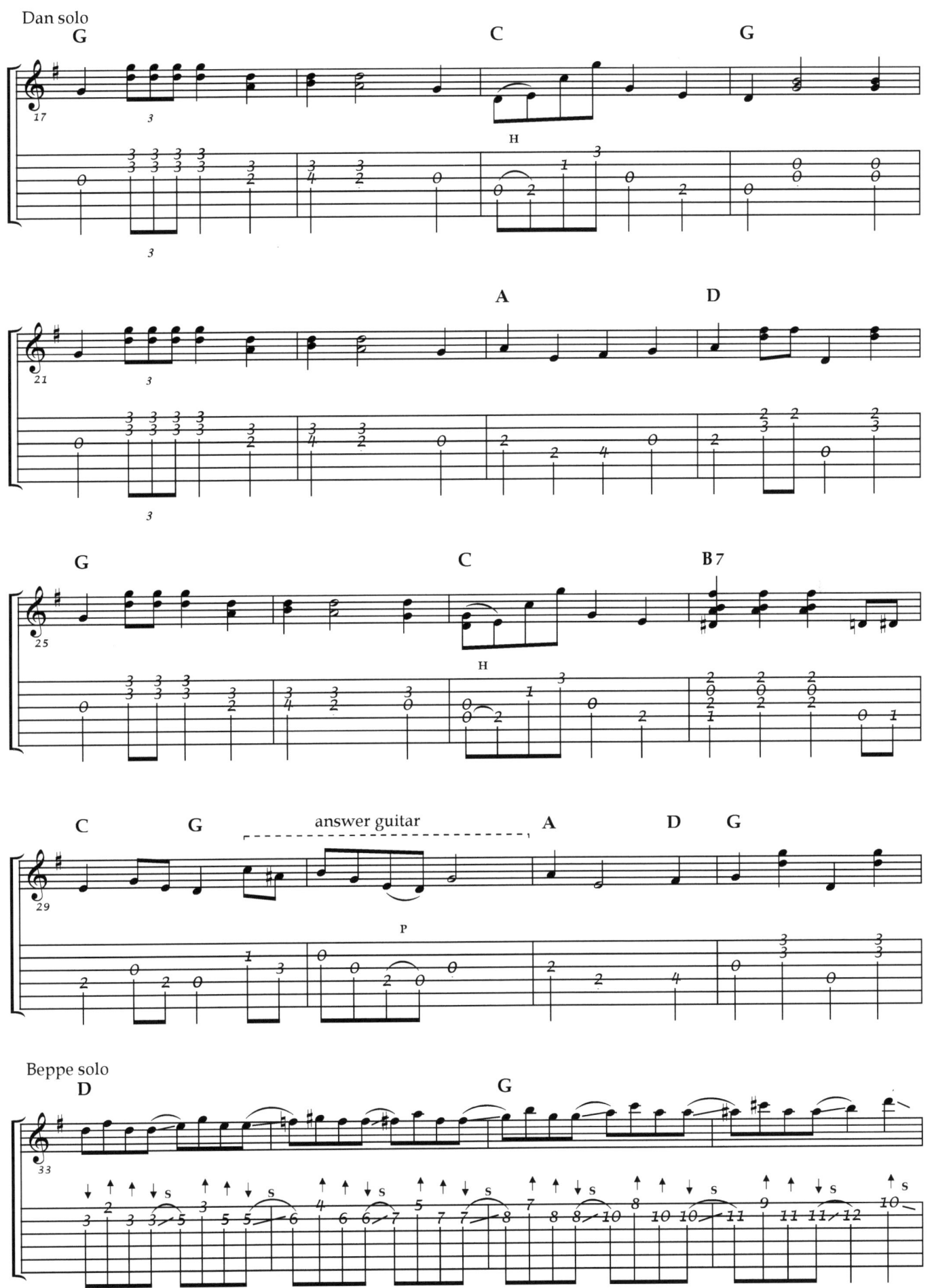

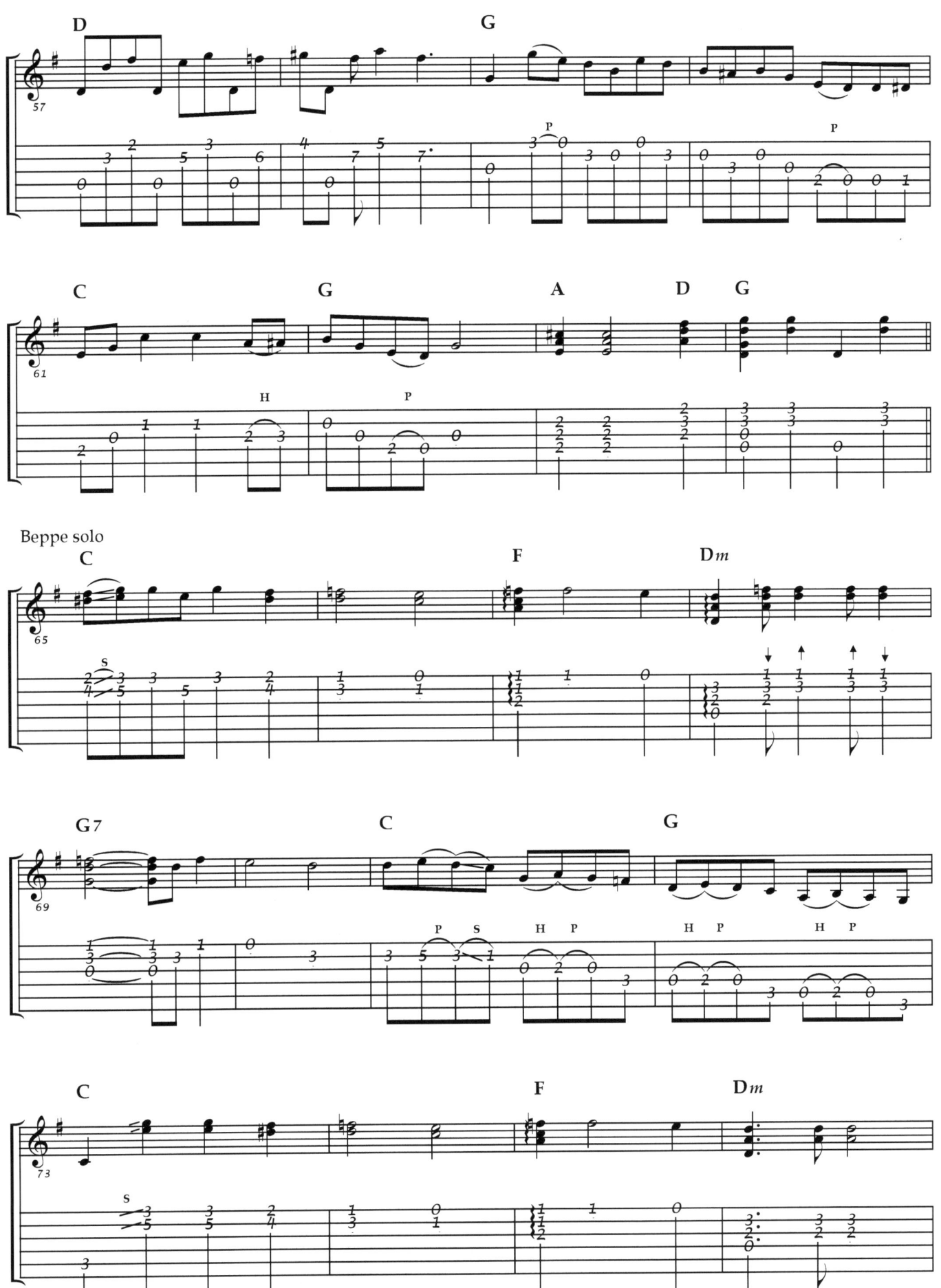

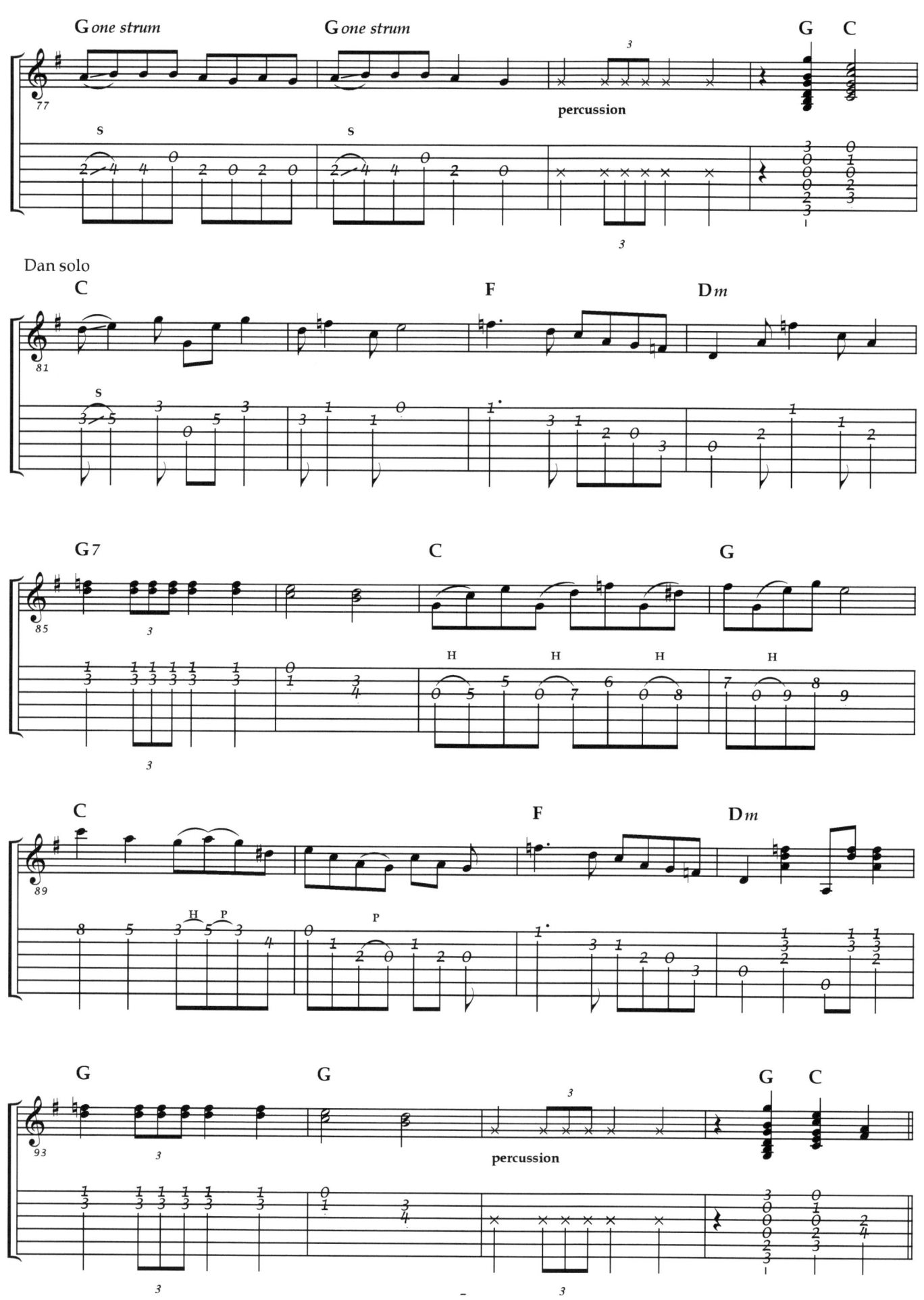

Under the Double Eagle

Traditional, arranged by Beppe Gambetta and Dan Crary

© 2002 Giuseppe Gambetta (SIAE - ITALY). All rights reserved. Used by permission.

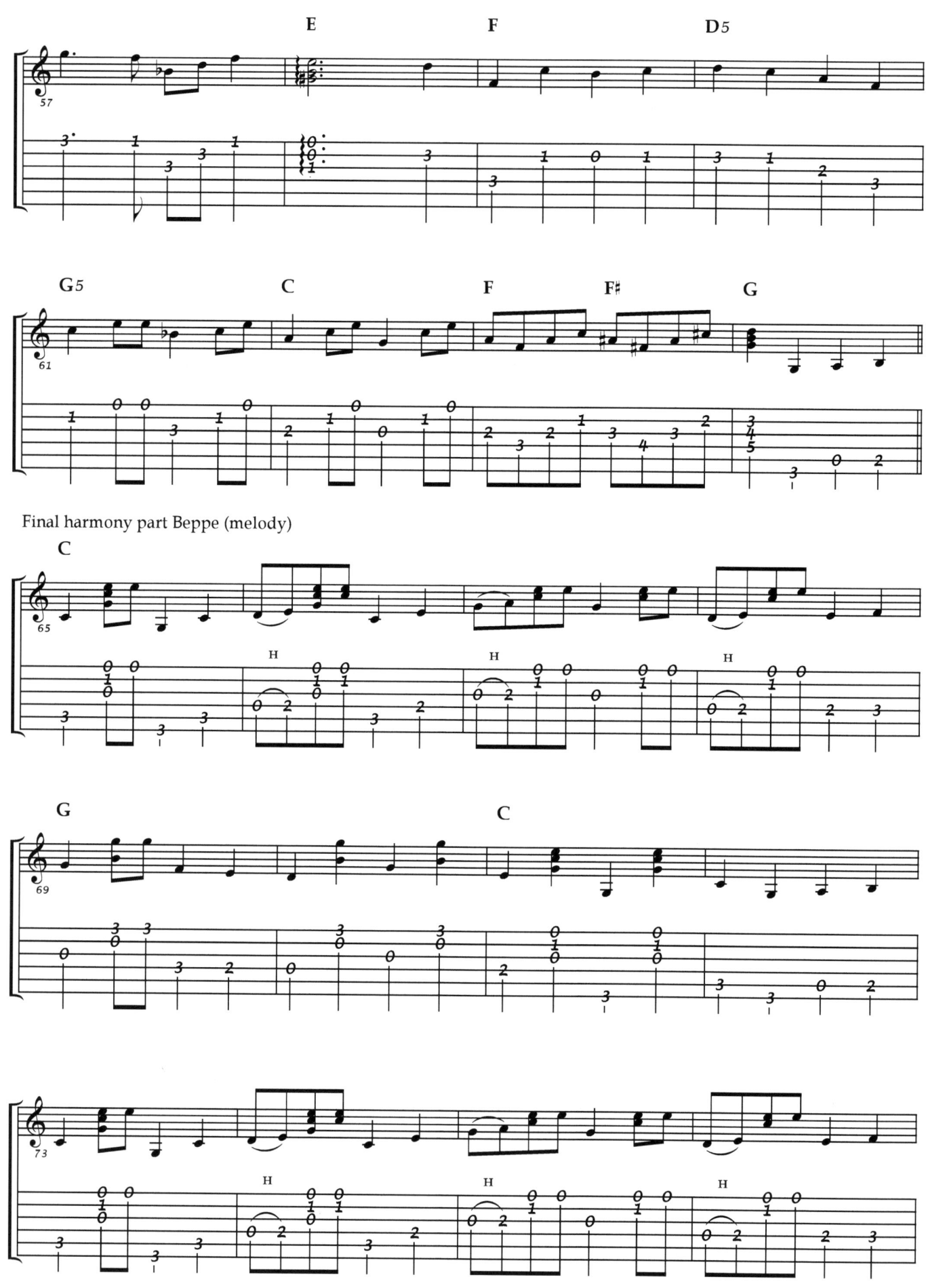

Final harmony part Beppe (melody)

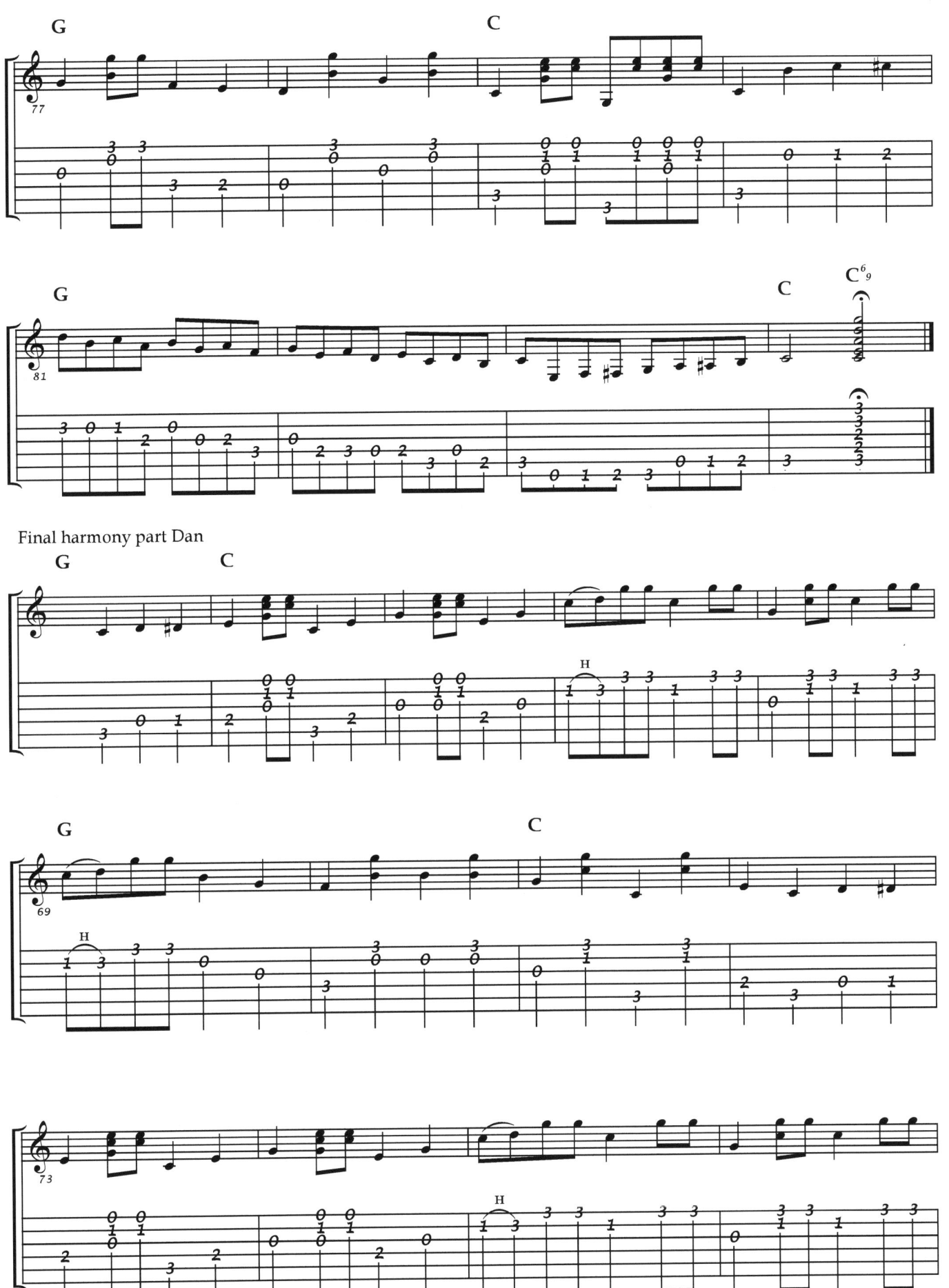

Final harmony part Dan

75

Red Shoes

Music by Beppe Gambetta

Tuning: D A D G B E

Capo V

♩ = 129

repeat the last
two measures
fading out

© 2002 Giuseppe Gambetta (SIAE - ITALY). All rights reserved. Used by permission.

Editing: TooMuch - www.toomuchgroup.com
Front cover photo by Costantino Costa
Back cover, page 11 and page 79 photos by Stefano Goldberg
Additional photos by Federica Calvino Prina

Many thanks to Roberto Dalla Vecchia, John Weingart,
Taylor Guitars, Elixir Strings.

UNIQUELY INTERESTING MUSIC!

Made in the USA
Charleston, SC
21 November 2010